Life-Is it God's *Or* Mine to End?

LESSONS FROM SEVEN MIRACLES

by

W Graham Monteith

Grosvenor House
Publishing Limited

All rights reserved
Copyright © W Graham Monteith, 2010

W Graham Monteith is hereby identified as author of this
work in accordance with Section 77 of the Copyright, Designs
and Patents Act 1988

The book cover picture is copyright to Inmagine Corp LLC

This book is published by
Grosvenor House Publishing Ltd
28-30 High Street, Guildford, Surrey, GU1 3HY.
www.grosvenorhousepublishing.co.uk

This book is sold subject to the conditions that it shall not, by way of
trade or otherwise, be lent, resold, hired out or otherwise circulated
without the author's or publisher's prior consent in any form of binding or
cover other than that in which it is published and
without a similar condition including this condition being imposed
on the subsequent purchaser.

A CIP record for this book
is available from the British Library

ISBN 978-1-907652-37-0

FOR
EDDIE AND JEAN LITTLE

Contents

Preface	vii
God's Value of Life	1
Which Miracles?	17
Our Mortal Bodies and Immortal Souls	31
Core Values of Life	43
'I am the Resurrection and the Life'	55
Our Value of Life and Death	74
To Cherish or Abandon Life	90
Re-stating God's Values	104
Epilogue	110
Bibliography	112

Preface

This book on the resurrection miracles is the second of which I hope might end up as a trilogy. It has always intrigued me that a large percentage of the gospels relate miracles of one kind or another which Jesus performed and from which he sometimes taught. In 2005, I published a book on the healing miracles. There is little point about writing about any of the miracles if they do not inform us of the way God intended us to respond to them.

In the case of the healing miracles, there has been a neglect of the disabled people who were affected by them and *Deconstructing Miracles: From Thoughtless Indifference to Honouring Disabled People* sought to show that those who were cured had a value which was reflected in the miracles but is often neglected by preachers and expositors. This current book seeks to relate the implied value of life which God chose to reveal in these seven miracles where someone is brought back to life and the way we ourselves treat life today. There is an urgency to continue to address the issue of euthanasia in new and hopefully innovative ways.

The third group of miracles are the nature miracles. These include feeding of crowds, walking on water and stilling the tempestuous waters of Galilee. What are we to make of them and what do they relate to this age. If I had the answer, I would already have outlined an embryonic book.

I have all the usual people to thank and trust that they will enjoy the end product of their labours. My main help came from the family. For the third time, I have to thank my mother-in-law, Jean Little, for typing most of the book to my dictation. Jason Wardley inspired me to look positively at death and to dabble in post-modernism.

I would also like to acknowledge all the authors and publishers who have been quoted in the course of the book. Without the stimulation of their ideas, nothing would have inspired me to write.

Edinburgh, 2010

Biblical quotations are from the *New International Version* (NIV) – International Bible Society, Copyright © 1973, 1978, 1984 by International Bible Society. They have been drawn from *Pradis* CD-ROM – Copyright © The Zondervan Corporation, 2002.

Chapter I

God's Value of Life

Christianity has a chance of becoming immortal as long as man stays mortal.

(Robert Ochs, 1969; p 7)

There can be absolutely no doubt that God values life. He, after all, created Adam and a companion for him in Eve with the expectation that they would procreate and populate the world which he saw as good. Even after the fall, God offered a new covenant with his people which is signified forever by the rainbow. In Jesus Christ, he offered eternal life and gave to men and women an assurance of the value of life which we have always yearned. Every one of us has at some time wished for immortality – death is a temporal inconvenience which we would love to see abolished without any consideration of religion or of salvation.

There is another fundamental example of God's commitment to social intercourse at the heart of the doctrine of the Trinity. Each of the three figures in the Godhead has its own identity – Father, Son and Holy Spirit. Each has an independent role in the ongoing narrative of creation, yet Jesus, the Son, has no ministry without reference to his Father's will, as in his prayer in the Garden of Gethsemane (Matthew 26: 36–46), or in his filial understanding of the law and its pure application. Similarly, the Holy Spirit is nothing without knowledge and acceptance of Jesus. The social dependence of each on the other lends weight to our conviction that created humankind has the greatest potential in a social context of values which disappear when every woman and man become mere atoms of individuality.

The question, 'does God value life?' is almost therefore superfluous. The real question must be what does God value in life? These values can only be found in a divinely ordained social setting. This is a tradition which is embedded in the scripture common to Judaism and Christianity, the four Gospels and the letters of the New Testament.

Are there clues in the Bible as to what God values and why it has been so important that we are given every opportunity to live our lives fully and in the grace of Jesus Christ? It will be argued in this book that miracles in which Jesus, Elisha or Elijah and Saint Paul in the Acts of Apostles, bring people back to life display the qualities which God wants us to understand as being valuable in life. In other words, it is not just the restoration of breath and movement that is important but all the issues which surround life which disappear in death.

Miracles and Restoration

There are seven miracles in which life is restored in the Old and New Testaments and it is important at the outset to try to define the restoration of life. Additionally, there are numerous references to raising the dead. To use the term resurrection is obviously the easiest and most straightforward way of describing these miracles. Yet resurrection is about the general resurrection at the end of time. Jesus' own resurrection is qualitatively different from all other 'resurrections' in that Jesus was not resurrected to continue his life where it had been cut short on Good Friday, but to show the glory of his new spiritual body to countless witnesses prior to his ascension. With his resurrection, Jesus had a new ministry and a new task to complete in the forty days before the ascension. With every other resurrection miracle, one common characteristic is that we do not know, or can only guess, how they spent the rest of their lives or how they faced ultimate death in old age or at any other time. For this reason, I am reluctant to use the word resurrection to describe these miracles. 'Resuscitation' has become a very clinical term yet is almost nearer the meaning we need. Perhaps a longer phrase is required: miracles in which life's vital signs are restored. The restoration of life is the restoration of the body's capacity to live life to the full both physically and spiritually. In short, these seven miracles are about restoring the life which God considers valuable to someone who had lost the vital signs of living.

In a previous book, *Deconstructing Miracles* (2005), I have argued that Jesus so redefined disability that he offered new life to those whom he touched in dynamic ways which restored their function within society and their personal worth. Whenever Jesus healed, he offered new opportunities in life. The person with a skin disease was allowed to rejoin society as a 'clean' person without the great ceremonies which had previously been demanded, and the stigma of blindness or paralysis was removed. In removing these stigmas, Jesus freed the disabled person from the bondage of either begging or family dependency and took away the suggestion that they were tainted by sin and brought their misfortune on themselves.

In a deeply religious society such stigmas excluded one from the religious observances which were so important to most in society. Blame and uncleanness cast people out of the synagogues to beg near where worshippers gathered. This is vividly illustrated in the healing of the disabled man at the Golden Gate. After he was healed by Peter and John, he entered the Temple shouting and dancing for joy because now he was restored to the heart of the cult. (Acts 3: 1 – 10) The reality of Jesus' ability to release people outweighs any doubts we may have about the true nature of the miracles. Magicians abounded at the time of Jesus and they offered temporary cures which had no consideration of the impact upon the disabled person but were very concerned for the effect on the onlooker. In Jesus' case the miracle was person-centred and always addressed the need to overcome guilt and the weight of an oppressive society which traditionally despised illness and its victims. Pilch (1995) argues that Mediterranean society, which included Palestine, was characterized by an all-pervading culture of honour and shame.

Stigma always makes people more isolated. They tend to be avoided by people and excluded from normal everyday life. This tends to build up a sense of shame which can be reinforced by prejudice and the customs of our society. Shame compounds the isolation and only by the removal of the stigma and the public freeing of the individual from his or her guilt can he or she be restored to any kind of normality. Illness brings with it burdens which can only be lifted by relating to the person.

The medicine of the time prolonged suffering whilst Jesus went straight to the nub of the matter. Whilst symptoms could be alleviated by many, Jesus brought the narrative of suffering to an end by restoring the person to a new position in society where his experience of illness ceased to be simply 'one damn thing after another'. (Kleinman, 1988; p 232)

There is a temptation today to seek the same spectacular miracle as did these magicians, while forgetting the urgent need to tackle the injustice and indignity of unaddressed disability. The value at the end of one of Jesus' miracles was not just health but a full restoration of life itself. There is always an implied faith in the fullness and wholeness of life which suggests that Jesus, as Son of God, could place a value on the characteristics of life which most characterise the qualities of lives preparing for the coming Kingdom of God. It may be argued that Jesus offers a restoration to the type of life which his Father saw as important in the preparation of the Kingdom. The Kingdom, after all, was where the banquet was prepared and scorned by the rich and the fortunate but fully accepted by those who could be found in the byways and highways and included disabled people. (Luke 14:15–23)

If it is possible to find rejoicing and plenty in the Kingdom for those who were restored through healing, surely it is equally possible to understand that the dead were raised so that they might similarly enjoy the fruits of the Kingdom amongst them and the path to the Kingdom beyond our present awareness.

Contemporary valuations of life

It is very difficult to define death in the context of the Gospels. Death has been changing throughout the centuries and is doing so at a terrifying speed in this age. Peter Singer, the controversial medical ethicist who advocates euthanasia, is correct in arguing that the definition of death must always be updated. Singer argues that death is continually being redefined by medical science pushing the limits which maybe preserved as vital signs. (Singer, 2002) It is perfectly possible to keep a person in a persistent vegetative state alive for many years but Singer argues that in line with social contract thinking, from Rousseau to Rawls, society has no obligation to maintain the life of a person who can make no contribution whatsoever to society. As a utilitarian, Singer does not see happiness in the tragedy of a person left in a vegetative state, therefore euthanasia is justified. His views have been bluntly characterised thus by Susan Krantz:

> As an egoist, I "look out for number one" I relegate the interests [of others] to second place at best. Other persons are simply resources for my own project, and to be treated as my advantage dictates. (Krantz, 2002; p27)

The writers of the Gospels had little concept of 'brain death' or the ability to maintain the vital signs of life after a major cardiac arrest. In order to value life, one must now understand many aspects of life's qualities. Death is more than the absence of a pulse, more than the absence of condensation of breath on a mirror. With technology comes the power of the switch – to sustain life or to turn it off. And such a decision requires the courage to choose between the quality of an isolated, atomic, life or a life which has been part of many people's lives. Never has the debate about the quality of life been so acute in choosing its ending. The debate has expanded not simply to whether life is valuable but to the value of death also. Death to some now is a welcome relief, to others the process of dying is something which is fearful as they take account of poor nursing standards in homes and impersonal medical advances in hospitals. Many now wish to be reassured that they will not suffer the slow indignities which one in five will suffer in the absence of family and friends who would have surrounded them in earlier ages, in fact probably until sixty years ago. (Kellehear, 2007) If life is measured solely by dignity, those who advocate euthanasia have a certain truthful insight on their side. If, as this book argues, the miracles indicate many more qualities to life, individualistic considerations of dignity pale into insignificance. Dignity in death, which is a different topic, must however remain a paramount concern of the church.

In sum, to be restored to life bestows values on life which must be explored and understood in the context of the Gospels to counteract the seeming truthful insights of those who advocate euthanasia. The Gospels however, give no indication that euthanasia is acceptable and thus a more comprehensive account of these values must be gleaned from the miracles contained within the Bible's books.

The Value of Life

The aim of this book, however, is to look at the value of life. Modern fear of death has in some ways devalued life in that people become more concerned about a good death rather than a good life. What we want to discern is what makes a good life in the context of Christians living for the representation of the Kingdom on this earth and in eternity. A good life is one that imitates Christ through an understanding of his teachings, a determination to treat people as we discern how he dealt with his friends and those with whom he shared time and discourse, and the values he would have wished on those whom he brought back to life. These lives are important because they restore the opportunity of living to God's glory having once faced death.

Death may have been defined much more simply in earlier times than Singer does today but then life and medical knowledge were simpler. The absence of breath was a sign of death, as might be unconsciousness or extreme lack of colour. Death was not defined by medicine but by those who surrounded the dead relative or whatever. Just as stillness and a morbid lack of life may have signified death in less modern times, so life lived fully in a family setting, worshipping God and showing the love which Jesus exemplified was a sign of a full and wholesome life.

What we want to do is value life. There are many ways to doing this and many of them make no reference to religion, or more pertinently the life which is expected in the Kingdom of God, which is expected of Christians. In popular culture life tends to be valued not as a whole but as a transient phase such as celebrity success or money. Life is definitely preferable to death and is even celebrated in death itself. Don Cupitt (2003) argues that the entire linguistic emphasis in the average funeral has now moved from celebrating and looking forward to eternity to looking back and celebrating not just the life that is past but the life as if it is still present. Howarth (2007) reiterates, rather unconvincingly, that attitudes to death have become progressively more individualistic as the influence of Christianity has declined and pluralism has increased within society. I would argue that established religion has lost its element of social control and with this the individual has adopted a 'pick and mix' attitude to death. With such moves in popular sentiments life has become materialistic rather than spiritual.

However, all these images of life fail to accommodate those who are frail or disabled – so profoundly so that they cannot make much contribution to the life of society. The same is true of those who are dying or suffer from a terminal illness. A good, controlled death is much more preferable to a life of seeming suffering.

Within modern society there are groups who defend and seek to define the value of life against all these trends. But they tend to be working at the margins of life and it is arguable that secular society is drowning out any Christian attempt to define value in all lives. Nevertheless, it is at the margins of life that most effort must be put to defend the qualities of all life.

We shall look at two such movements. First, the determined effort of some political scientists and students of jurisprudence must be taken as an example. There has long been a lack of acceptance of the value of profoundly disabled people and a slow slide towards the utilitarian attitudes of Singer but it can also be seen in society's unwillingness to adequately reward carers, be they unpaid family members or part of the growing army of poorly paid, lowly esteemed and predominately female workforce in care homes and in the ordinary homes of disabled people in need. So undervalued are the lives of such disabled people that there has been a gradual erosion of any professionalism in their care, leaving it in the hands of students and those who are willing to work for a few pence more than a shop assistant or hotel chambermaids. It is very easy to protest against the treatment of these workers, but the truth is that there are not the resources within our society as it is presently structured to value them and those for whom they care.

Martha Nussbaum is one theorist who has defended both the rights of disabled people and their caregivers, to use her preferred word. She criticises those theorists who build upon the idea of a 'social contract'. Such a contract demands of everyone a contribution towards society. People and their place in society by their contribution to it are esteemed by the extent and value of that contribution. Rawls is the chief proponent of such a theory and his theory of justice has been respected by many for a long time. Nussbaum is no exception in her admiration for his work but she argues that he has overlooked people who cannot make a visible contribution to society and are dependent on their caregivers for every aspect of life. She argues that:

... nobody is ever self-efficient, the independence we enjoy is always both temporary and partial, and it is good to be reminded of that fact by a theory that alas stresses the importance of care in times of dependency. But is being "some mother's child" a sufficient image for the citizen in a just society? (And is care a sufficient image for motherhood?) I think we need a lot more liberty and opportunity, *the chance to form a plan of life*, the chance to learn and imagine on one's own, the chance to form friendships and other political relationships that are chosen and not merely given. (Nussbaum, 2006; p 219f)

Nussbaum has a concern that society has an obligation to respect and nurture human dignity as she develops an Aristotelian model of care. The quality of care given is an implicit indicator of the value of a life, especially if it is care given with love by a family member. But Nussbaum moved on to suggest that the carer should offer a person a life plan and opportunity to develop whatever capabilities maybe within him or her. Many profoundly disabled people are given the opportunity to develop a dream plan consisting of the things that are mostly likely to make them happy and thus offer happiness to those around them. The lives of such people should be lived to the fullness of their capabilities. By stressing this important aspect of life, Nussbaum corrects the weakness of the liberal theory that we can all, we must all make contributions of our own to society. If we can do so with the help of care, life takes on an infinitely stronger value and is worth living fully. Every life has potential as long as vital signs remain and people surround it with personhood.

Second, there are the pro-life groups. These are mainly religious people as they have on their side most interpretations of scripture, not only of the Gospels but of the books of the Old Testament which are held in common with Jews and Muslims. The pro-life lobby goes far beyond the argument of this book into areas such as stem cell research and the less exotic applications of cloning and the preservation (and destruction) of frozen embryos. Our concern here is the preservation of the very lives which are going to demand high levels of care. I am not going to recite the Roman Catholic doctrines opposing abortion and euthanasia here but discuss rather Vanier's attitude to lives which have been preserved. In an article in the *Globe and Mail* (Toronto, November 29, 2008), he graciously defends the right of Canada to honour a distinguished pro-abortionist for his life's dedication to the rights of women and their welfare but goes on to argue that the act of abortion demeans the sexual act and undermines its chief aim of procreation, which is a very Catholic doctrine. To find Vanier's true contribution to an understanding of the value of life we have to look elsewhere and much deeper than that of the average pro-life campaigner.

> [The] mystery of love is central to the communal vision of l'Arche, which seeks to overcome the barriers between people through building relationships and friendships of mutuality, and through the practices of welcoming the stranger and the needy. For Vanier, the human journey proceeds from loneliness and rejection (due to fear) to belonging, from exclusion to inclusion, from brokenness to community, from oppression to liberation, through paths of healing, forgiveness, and freedom. (Yong, 2007; p 202)

Amos Yong argues very cogently that Vanier has spent many years of his life trying to re-define our acceptance of disability and Down syndrome in particular. Statistics in recent research have suggested that the number of foetuses being aborted because of suspected Down syndrome has fallen compared to a decade ago in England and Wales. (*The National Down Syndrome Cytogenetic Register: 2006 Annual Report*) This may be explained by the growing understanding of the high quality of life which a child with this disability can offer to parents and the opportunities which will follow in later life. Jean Vanier has devoted his life to caring for disabled people with the most profound disabilities in communities throughout the world, which transcend creedal boundaries and where opportunities exist for volunteers, familiar carers and disabled people to come together in accepting communities.

This is where Yong identifies l'Arche's unique understanding of the value of life. People who are rejected by society are accepted into these communities and into a new wholeness which may either have been lacking or cannot be sustained at home. The degree of acceptance is a sign of Christ at work as he spent his earthly ministry accepting people and offering them value. Members of L'Arche begin to assume value as they are accepted by the strength and fortitude of those who not only volunteer but become part of the new world order in which weakness becomes strength and life becomes valuable, even if their only contribution is a smile.

The difficulty I have with Vanier's movement is that it tends to glamorize disability and to make a virtue out of the care which is offered which takes on a spiritual dimension which is almost unhealthy. Disability may become valued for disability's sake. The broken body is treated too much as a symbol of Christ's body and the carer's service becomes too much of a religious duty. I was shocked when I was led to believe that disabled pilgrims to Lourdes are stripped naked and manhandled through the waters which make the town famous. It is as if the exposure of the disabled body is in come way akin to the exposure of Christ's body as it is portrayed in so many paintings after being taken down from the cross. In these paintings, Christ has at least a loin cloth! There is something of Catholic piety in such attitudes which threaten to hold disabled people back. One never hears a talk by Vanier on the advances in technology which are offering the most profoundly disabled opportunities to communicate and to gain some degree of independence beyond the imaginings of carers who find their present situation perfectly acceptable.

Several writers have brought together the work of Nussbaum and Vanier in a Christian theory of friendship and disability. They have built a model of 'solicitous caring'. They argue that what disabled people most require is the gift of friendship and acceptance in a world which can ignore them. Authors like

John Swinton (2001) and Hans Reinders (2008) believe that such care must be offered as an imitation of Christ whose acceptance of the marginalised was one essence of the Gospels. When such care is offered, an implicit value is put upon the lives of those who are touched and the obvious influence of Christ shows yet again God's value and, concern for life. John Swinton begins one book with an emphatic statement of purpose and challenge to the church – 'This is a book about radical friendship.' The church should remember, and act upon Jesus' chosen friendships with the poor and socially outcast. Many of those with mental health problems are homeless or economically disenfranchised, i.e. poor. Jesus makes a bias towards their needs imperative. Furthermore, our lack of understanding of schizophrenics and people with other such conditions makes them strangers, others, to the Christian community. In an eloquent use of Aristotelian concepts of virtue and friendship, we should approach such friendships in a deeply solicitous way. He continues that "radical" Christ-centred friendship ...

> ... demands that the church become a community that is deeply committed to those who are, in some senses, "least like us." It demands that we sit with the poor, commune with the marginalised, and sojourn with those whom society despises. (2001: p 51)

What we must discover is a way of describing the value of life which embraces everyone. Life is valuable, period. It should not be the case that we must go to the margins to discover value in life. Rather we should seek out universal values which are explicit and not implicitly illustrated by our treatment of those on the margin who are valued by the principled actions of some well intentioned people, or are protected by law when they have an egotistical desire to end a life which has ceased to have value in their estimation. There is something profoundly depressing in the spectre of people who are prepared to cut the final social ties with both loved ones and the caring professions.

Miracles defined

It is proposed to examine the miracles where people are brought back from death to life as a way of discovering how God valued life. The miracles themselves will be taken as given and apart from a mention in the review of literature, no attempt will be made to explain them. Such explanations would touch upon the role of resuscitation and would ask whether those performing such miracles were ahead of their time. Nor will the cultural context of the miracles be examined. It is true that Jesus was making a statement about current religious practices when he performed such miracles but that is not important in this context.

I think it is important to understand what a miracle may mean. There are firm limits to what we may infer from them. For instance, the allegorical approach may be a good way to produce sermons but it can lead to an abuse of the meaning and purpose of Jesus in performing a miracle. Likewise, certain evangelical evaluations detract from the human interest, as opposed to the divine, in the stories. Corner discusses at length the philosophical approaches to miracles and is critical of David Hume's understanding of them as impossible violations of natural laws. Many other philosophical approaches have limitations and he is naturally forced to offer his own definition:

> I will therefore define a 'miracle' as a special or immediate act of God, as opposed to God's continuous work of creating and sustaining the world. The result of this act will be beneficial and religiously significant. (Corner, 2005; p 15).

This definition is useful in that it allows us to build a theory of God's moral authority and intentions. God's prime statement is firmly rooted in creation which is where this book started. The world is good in all aspects but with the fall imperfections crept into the wider picture. Thus death was not an ally but an enemy to be feared. Likewise, illness and disability were to be feared and where fear exists, discrimination and labelling follows. Jesus demonstrates his abhorrence at such exclusiveness by large sections of the society in which he lived.

Therefore, it is possible to expand Corner's definition a little further by seeing *God's actions through miracles as postscripts to his act of creation*. The narrative grows and evolves as God redeems situations which were not to be found in the Garden of Eden. God corrects not only man but the imbalance which he has created by showing how better ways can be achieved as a result of his miracles. Thus, my definition allows for a moral dimension to be shown by God's miracles and by those which involve raising the dead in particular. In this instance, mortality is shown in a new light and life as it is lived is given its values.

Life restored – Mortality remains

Each of these miracles took place amid social circumstances. Invariably, it was a family member who had died. Often there was evidence of poverty and of a trusting desire to place one's fate in the hands of Jesus or the Old Testament prophets. By looking at the nature of the life which has been lost and was restored, it may be possible to point to the value which God put on their life and by speculating about the ongoing life of the person who has been brought back from the dead, it may be possible to find value in the life that was going to be lived until the it ended in death. It cannot be repeated enough that those who were brought back to life were still going to die sometime. This is why the opening quotation from Ochs is so important. Those who were brought back to life were not brought back to immortality but to mortality. They would still have to face death some day but with the knowledge that their lives had assumed certain values in the miracle which had been performed. Ochs, taking his arguments from Karl Rahner, explains how life is a journey through time which is delineated by death. Man cannot do anything to mitigate or alter the fact of death as he can many other natural phenomena. Salvation can be accepted by coming to terms with death, redefined by the death and resurrection of Jesus. Life is characterised by *concupiscientia*, which can be translated either as 'unbridled lust' or 'the soul searching for communion with God'. In this context it is the latter that is appropriate. Man's journey is a mortal one but with a right understanding of death can eventually be freed by the salvation of Christ.

There is one matter that must be cleared up early in this book. At no point should it be taken that Jesus performed miracles just so that people might lead lives of faith. Jesus accepted that those who benefited from miracles might not find faith. Indeed in the story of the healing of ten lepers only one returned 'praising God in a loud voice' and offering thanks. There may be a lesson in that he was a Samaritan. Jesus uncharacteristically expresses disappointment that he is the only one of the ten to return. (Luke 17: 11–19) He may well have regarded his mission as gathering the lost sheep of Israel but it was quite conceivable that some might not respond either to his teaching or his miracles.

The obvious first task must be to identify the miracles concerned and to comment on them in the context of the many hermeneutics which have emerged from their study. Next, we can look at the individual miracles in detail, their common traits, and values. After this it must be asked what a living body actually implies. The fact that we have mortal bodies exposes us to different kinds of frailty and makes us aware that even in death there are rituals and conditions attached to our longing for resurrection. Since this book is mainly about restoration, a chapter will be devoted to the values which are restored when a character in the Bible is brought back to life and the nature of God's aspiration for our lives as mortal individuals. Since the raising of Lazarus presents the most theological of the miracles more space will be devoted to it. Jesus here presents a full picture of the miracle of resurrection and the mode of its revelation in his own life and teaching.

By a close examination of the implications of the miracles of resuscitation, I contend that we can see what values God would like to see in our lives and what he offers to us when we accept his covenant with us in Jesus Christ. The tension of being mortal but seeking immortality through salvation in Jesus will be initially focussed on the lives of those whom Jesus rescued from premature death. They act as a metaphor for all our lives.

Chapter II

Which Miracles?

In this chapter we will look at precisely what miracles there are in the Bible which deal with the 'raising of the dead'. These miracles have lent themselves to many theories which variously seek to explain how the dead could be raised or what allegorical lessons may be learnt from the actions and circumstances surrounding such miracles. Whilst both of these approaches have value, what we wish to discover is the values which were portrayed as belonging to God in his valuing of life. These values will be teased out in a later chapter but at the moment it is important that we continue to establish God's essential interest in life and how it is conducted.

Jesus leaves us in little doubt that he considers it important that life be preserved, be restored when confronted by tragic circumstances of a daughter's death or the brother of a dearly beloved family, Lazarus. Jesus commissioned his disciples and followers on many occasions and demanded of them both psychological understanding of people and to be skilled in healing which they probably never dreamt they had. They were only to be achieved by the intervention of the Holy Spirit on whom he taught his disciples to depend, most explicitly in John chapter 13 in his great discourse on the coming of the Paraclete after his death. Specific to our concerns, in Matthew 10, verse 8 Jesus commanded and prepared his disciples for a tough and austere ministry:

> Heal the sick, raise the dead, cleanse those who have leprosy, drive out demons. Freely you have received, freely give.

In his coded message to John the Baptist (Luke 7: 22), Jesus had made it clear that his healings were a sign of the kingdom to come and now in this commission he adds 'raising the dead' to the list of actions expected of his disciples. Yet such miracles are rare in the New Testament and suggest that Jesus either did not perform them very often or that they had a very special role. Each of them contained a message which meant a lot within the culture of the time and underscored values which had already been witnessed in the Old Testament. It might be argued that Jesus was following in the footsteps of the great prophets, Elijah and Elisha, in the scriptures upon which so much of his teaching depended and developed.

There are numerous interpretations of the miracles of raising of the dead in the gospels. Bolt (2003) offers one such suggesting that the writer of the gospel of Mark had a strong desire to emphasise Jesus' victory over death by showing how prevalent attitudes were to death even in illness. Death was associated with demons, spirits who could bring evil in death as in life. Bolt argues that some forms of illness were seen as living deaths. The emaciated bodies of 'lepers' were a stark reminder of the closeness of death whilst blindness was seen by many in the Hellenistic world as a living death. Such a view is not acceptable to the modern mind which accepts that disabled people can have a great quality of life. Bolt argues that because Jesus could overcome the demons which caused these illnesses and bring the blind back from the living death that they were supposed to suffer, that Jesus had conquered death in his ministry before his own struggle with death upon the cross.

Death was a constant fear and always near to a people who were brutalised by Roman occupation and whatever attitude to death may be adopted, the resurrection of Jesus was a victory at a time of very great oppression.

The miracles of Elijah and Elisha are the main two instances of the raising of the dead in the Old Testament. However, there is a debate about the extent of belief in the resurrection in the Old Testament communities. It was generally regarded that one went to Sheol upon death and the only testimony of immortality was people's memory of you and in the case of so many biblical characters, the great deeds which they had wrought. Some scholars argue that there was a much greater expectation of resurrection than has sometimes been suggested. Levenson (2006) is one such who argues that modern Judaism has a great desire to seek intimations of immortality in their scriptures.

Apart from the miracles there are two references to resurrection: the valley of dry bones in Ezekiel 37:1–14 is the most vivid passage but a more complicated example is additionally found in Daniel 12: 1–3:

1. "At that time Michael, the great prince who protects your people, will arise. There will be a time of distress such as has not happened from the beginning of nations until then. But at that time your people—everyone whose name is found written in the book—will be delivered.
2. Multitudes who sleep in the dust of the earth will awake: some to everlasting life, others to shame and everlasting contempt.
3. Those who are wise will shine like the brightness of the heavens, and those who lead many to righteousness, like the stars for ever and ever.

Ezekiel chapter 15 is one of the most poetic parables in the entire Bible and relates the story of a valley strewn with dry bones which come together into living bodies at the behest of God who breathes life into them. It is generally agreed that this is not an account of resurrection but a poetic representation of the devastated state of Israel after the exile. Eichrodt (1970) illustrates the ambiguous exegesis of the passage by emphasising God's domination of life in that despite the parabolic nature of the story, it is illustrated that God can bring life into every situation. Eichrodt does not quite read a resurrection miracle into the story but does emphasis the dominion of God which is shown to all in the incarnation of Jesus Christ. This is likewise accepted by Levenson who is more concerned however with the attitudes of Jewish readers.

Levenson later turns his attention to Daniel and argues that by the time this apocalyptic book was written there was a general

19

expectation that the righteous would be judged and raised at the general resurrection at the end of time. (Levenson, 2006; p 196ff) Such an image could easily be understood and adopted by early Christians and further developed by them throughout the ages. The words of Daniel do look forward to a much more dynamic relationship between the dead and their fate in the day of judgement, which is firmly part of Christian doctrine. (See also Grabbe, 1997.)

I Kings 17:17–24 – Elijah

17. Some time later the son of the woman who owned the house became ill. He grew worse and worse, and finally stopped breathing.
18. She said to Elijah, "What do you have against me, man of God? Did you come to remind me of my sin and kill my son?"
19. "Give me your son," Elijah replied. He took him from her arms, carried him to the upper room where he was staying, and laid him on his bed.
20. Then he cried out to the LORD, "O LORD my God, have you brought tragedy also upon this widow I am staying with, by causing her son to die?"
21. Then he stretched himself out on the boy three times and cried to the LORD, "O LORD my God, let this boy's life return to him!"
22. The LORD heard Elijah's cry, and the boy's life returned to him, and he lived.
23. Elijah picked up the child and carried him down from the room into the house. He gave him to his mother and said, "Look, your son is alive!"
24. Then the woman said to Elijah, "Now I know that you are a man of God and that the word of the LORD from your mouth is the truth."

Elijah had experienced the famine which beset the land in which he lived and had his ministry. He lodged with the widow of Zarephath and shared her family's subsistence rations which miraculously never ran out. He was well aware of the misery of poverty and the dependence of small family groups to stay close at such times of hardship. Not only was a child lost but a widow had lost her son who would have worked to help maintain subsistence within the household. Thus at one level this miracle is about poverty. At another level it was about the emotions of a mother who could not understand why the hospitality offered to a 'man of God' should result in such a terrible fate. Elijah was in some way mitigating the sorrow and anger of the widow by intervening.

The nature of the healing is not really our concern but cannot be overlooked. John Gray (1963; p 342) suggests that the method of healing was characteristic of a shaman who by bringing about bodily contact with the deceased took upon himself the disease. Such an interpretation is different from the belief I have long held that this was an early example of modern resuscitation technique. It mattered not save to note that breath was restored to the little boy.

The nature of Elijah's motivation is part of the narrative of how God values life and some issues will be revisited later.

2 Kings 4:17–37 - Elisha

17. But the woman became pregnant, and the next year about that same time she gave birth to a son, just as Elisha had told her.
18. The child grew, and one day he went out to his father, who was with the reapers.
19. "My head! My head!" he said to his father.

His father told a servant, "Carry him to his mother."

20. After the servant had lifted him up and carried him to his mother, the boy sat on her lap until noon, and then he died.
21. She went up and laid him on the bed of the man of God, then shut the door and went out.
22. She called her husband and said, "Please send me one of the servants and a donkey so I can go to the man of God quickly and return."
23. "Why go to him today?" he asked. "It's not the New Moon or the Sabbath."

"It's all right," she said.

LIFE-IS IT GOD'S OR MINE TO END?

24. She saddled the donkey and said to her servant, "Lead on; don't slow down for me unless I tell you."

25. So she set out and came to the man of God at Mount Carmel. When he saw her in the distance, the man of God said to his servant Gehazi, "Look! There's the Shunammite!

26. Run to meet her and ask her, 'Are you all right? Is your husband all right? Is your child all right?' "

"Everything is all right," she said.

27. When she reached the man of God at the mountain, she took hold of his feet. Gehazi came over to push her away, but the man of God said, "Leave her alone! She is in bitter distress, but the LORD has hidden it from me and has not told me why."

28. "Did I ask you for a son, my lord?" she said. "Didn't I tell you, 'Don't raise my hopes'?"

29. Elisha said to Gehazi, "Tuck your cloak into your belt, take my staff in your hand and run. If you meet anyone, do not greet him, and if anyone greets you, do not answer. Lay my staff on the boy's face."

30. But the child's mother said, "As surely as the LORD lives and as you live, I will not leave you." So he got up and followed her.

31. Gehazi went on ahead and laid the staff on the boy's face, but there was no sound or response. So Gehazi went back to meet Elisha and told him, "The boy has not awakened."

32. When Elisha reached the house, there was the boy lying dead on his couch.

33. He went in, shut the door on the two of them and prayed to the LORD.

34. Then he got on the bed and lay upon the boy, mouth to mouth, eyes to eyes, hands to hands. As he stretched himself out upon him, the boy's body grew warm.

35. Elisha turned away and walked back and forth in the room and then got on the bed and stretched out upon him once more. The boy sneezed seven times and opened his eyes.

36. Elisha summoned Gehazi and said, "Call the Shunammite." And he did. When she came, he said, "Take your son."

37. She came in, fell at his feet and bowed to the ground. Then she took her son and went out.

This story has quite a number of differences from the miracle involving Elijah. Elisha's resuscitation of this little boy is almost a mirror image of that miracle recorded in 1st Kings. The story is really longer than the verses quoted and actually begins at verse 8. It is interesting that in both miracles, the presence of the prophets ensure that provisions do not run out. In the case of Elijah he ensures that many neighbours have a plentiful supply of oil which never seems to run out. These miracles prefigure the feeding of the five thousand by Jesus. Nevertheless, in this case the woman is well to do and has a husband. She lacked a child which she was blessed with a year into the story. She came from Shunem and thus was a Shunammite. It is interesting that her origin singled out as Shunem is quite an important village in the books of Kings. The name lent itself to a practice which David adopted and is known as shunamitism whereby a young virgin was supposed to lie with an old man to give him warmth and energy to recover. The story of David's practice is found in I Kings 1:1. (Shapin & Martyn, 2000; p 1580) In other words, there is a strong element of symbolism about the renewal of life.

In this account of the miracle, we are given the symptoms of the illness: the boy had headaches which he reported to his father in the fields. We also have a concern that all appropriate rituals be carried out such as calling Elisha on the Sabbath or during a full moon phase and the body is laid out in a separate room, Elisha's room, as was common in those days and even to the present. Again the method of resuscitation is much more elaborately spelt out in this story as is the mode of the boy's revival. This story is one which introduces the importance of mourning which is of the essence in the next miracle to be discussed.

It seems best to leave the miracles of Jesus until last and so we turn to the Acts of the Apostles and the two miracles which emphasise the power of the Apostles through Jesus Christ over life and death.

Acts of the Apostles 9: 36–42 – Peter

> 36. In Joppa there was a disciple named Tabitha (which, when translated, is Dorcas), who was always doing good and helping the poor.

37. About that time she became sick and died, and her body was washed and placed in an upstairs room.

38. Lydda was near Joppa; so when the disciples heard that Peter was in Lydda, they sent two men to him and urged him, "Please come at once!"

39. Peter went with them, and when he arrived he was taken upstairs to the room. All the widows stood around him, crying and showing him the robes and other clothing that Dorcas had made while she was still with them.

40. Peter sent them all out of the room; then he got down on his knees and prayed. Turning toward the dead woman, he said, "Tabitha, get up." She opened her eyes, and seeing Peter she sat up.

41. He took her by the hand and helped her to her feet. Then he called the believers and the widows and presented her to them alive.

42. This became known all over Joppa, and many people believed in the Lord.

The most important point to highlight in this story of Tabitha is the mourning ritual which involved the women who had presumably followed her as a disciple. They were widows who were used to bereavement. It was they who laid out the body and who wept around the personal effects of the dead teacher, Tabitha or Dorcas. The importance of the family will be discussed later but the pathos of the sorority gathered around this iconic woman must be noted and the lack of ritual which was employed by Peter is an impressive departure from the miracles in the Gospels and even the Old Testament. Peter only prayed opposite her body.

Acts of the Apostles 20: 7–12 – Paul

7. On the first day of the week we came together to break bread. Paul spoke to the people and, because he intended to leave the next day, kept on talking until midnight.

8. There were many lamps in the upstairs room where we were meeting.

9. Seated in a window was a young man named Eutychus, who was sinking into a deep sleep as Paul talked on and on. When he was sound asleep, he fell to the ground from the third story and was picked up dead.

10. Paul went down, threw himself on the young man and put his arms around him. "Don't be alarmed," he said. "He's alive!"

11. Then he went upstairs again and broke bread and ate. After talking until daylight, he left.
12. The people took the young man home alive and were greatly comforted.

The resuscitation of Eutychus takes place within the context of worship and the incident happened close to dawn. There is a certain humour in this story in that Eutychus fell asleep while Paul preached on and on. We have all succumbed to dozing off during a sermon but very few of us have had the misfortune of sitting by an open window. Paul revived the young man as others have done by contact and having assured that he was again alive they continued the service with the breaking of bread. Bovon showed that many scholars have associated this miracle with worship and liturgy. He argues, in common with others quoted, that Luke was seeking to show that something special could happen during the common meals, some might say the Eucharist, which early Christians held. (Bovon, 2006; 435) The meal at Emmaus revealed the presence of Christ in the breaking of bread and the discussion of the events leading up to the death and resurrection of Jesus. Other examples may also be quoted.

This is important because it is good to see an association between worship, fellowship and belief and the preservation of life. Paul had previously carried out miracles which had led to a faith in his power and ability. These miracles were confirmation of his conversion from orthodox Judaism.

Jesus

Strangely, Jesus only raised three people from the dead in the course of his recorded ministry although many others are said to have taken place. Each of the gospels records one such example and Mark and Luke duplicate the story of Jairus' daughter. Matthew does not name the family but there is a strong suggestion that it is the same girl as mentioned in the other gospels.

In the case of John, a totally different structure and purpose to the story of the raising of Lazarus occurs. In this great chapter of John, Jesus utters one of his 'I am' sayings and for this reason the story will be dealt with in another chapter.

Luke 7:11–15

11. Soon afterward, Jesus went to a town called Nain, and his disciples and a large crowd went along with him.
12. As he approached the town gate, a dead person was being carried out—the only son of his mother, and she was a widow. And a large crowd from the town was with her.
13. When the Lord saw her, his heart went out to her and he said, "Don't cry."
14. Then he went up and touched the coffin, and those carrying it stood still. He said, "Young man, I say to you, get up!"
15. The dead man sat up and began to talk, and Jesus gave him back to his mother.

Jesus' encounter with a funeral party in Nain is the first time we have encountered death at its penultimate stage. A funeral is a time of ceremony and farewell but Jesus interrupts it and commands the boy to rise from the coffin. Not for the first time the miracle takes place in an atmosphere of family mourning. Nain is very close to Shunem which is the village where Elisha performed his miracle and the coincidence was not lost on the crowd who thought a new Messiah was in their midst.

Matthew 9:18–19 and 23–25

18. While he was saying this, a ruler came and knelt before him and said, "My daughter has just died. But come and put your hand on her, and she will live."
19. Jesus got up and went with him, and so did his disciples.
23. When Jesus entered the ruler's house and saw the flute players and the noisy crowd, 24 he said, "Go away. The girl is not dead but asleep." But they laughed at him.
25. After the crowd had been put outside, he went in and took the girl by the hand, and she got up.

In the synoptic gospels, Jesus only raises the young from the dead. It is hard to know why this is and nothing of great significance should be read into this. Matthew's story is about a ruler who begs Jesus to come and restore his daughter to life. The ruler may have been of the Jewish faith or possibly even a Roman but he threw himself on the mercy of Jesus who typically was some distance from the ruler's house. The story is then curiously interrupted in verses 20-22 by the account of the woman with a haemorrhage. Possibly this is because Matthew wanted to stress the faith of both the ruler and the woman who touches the 'edge of his cloak'. Modern hermeneutics tend to stress the faith of the ruler and his insistence that the presence of Jesus will revive his daughter. Her death is set in the busy milieu of the family home already hectically and noisily mourning. Jesus performs the miracle in quietness having dismissed the throngs from around him. Not for the first time in our examination of these miracles has the family proved important as both supplicants and mourners but only in the ultimate context of peaceful prayer and gentleness of the healing touch of Jesus.

The next two accounts of the return to life of the little girl belonging to the ruler of the synagogue are so like the story of the ruler's daughter in Matthew that there is every reason for treating these three stories similarly. All that has already been said about Matthew's account can apply to these but much more can be added. First, the ruler is undoubtedly a Jew, the leader of the synagogue. He carried much authority which is neatly contrasted with that of Jesus. The former had temporal authority; Jesus has divine authority from his Father. Previously, in the gospels of Matthew and Luke, there is a much more vivid example of this when Jesus helps the sick relative of a centurion who openly contrasts his absolute and arbitrary authority with that which he perceives to be held by the presence of Jesus. (Matthew 8:5–13 and Luke 7:1–10)

These two miracles show the broad spectrum of society to which Jesus appealed and held sway. His ministry and gospel extended not only to Samaritans but also to all factions of the household of Israel and even to Romans. His authority was widely accepted and many different types of people were brought to faith and offered the path to salvation.

Parallel Miracles

Mark 5:22–24, 35–43

22. Then one of the synagogue rulers, named Jairus, came there. Seeing Jesus, he fell at his feet
23. and pleaded earnestly with him, "My little daughter is dying. Please come and put your hands on her so that she will be healed and live."
24. So Jesus went with him. A large crowd followed and pressed around him.
35. While Jesus was still speaking, some men came from the house of Jairus, the synagogue ruler. "Your daughter is dead," they said. "Why bother the teacher any more?"
36. Ignoring what they said, Jesus told the synagogue ruler, "Don't be afraid; just believe."
37. He did not let anyone follow him except Peter, James and John the brother of James.
38. When they came to the home of the synagogue ruler, Jesus saw a commotion, with people crying and wailing loudly.
39. He went in and said to them, "Why all this commotion and wailing? The child is not dead but asleep." 40 But they laughed at him.

After he put them all out, he took the child's father and mother and the disciples who were with him, and went in where the child was.

41. He took her by the hand and said to her, "Talitha koum!" (which means, "Little girl, I say to you, get up!").

Luke 8:41–42, 49–56

42. Immediately the girl stood up and walked around (she was twelve years old). At this they were completely astonished.

41. Then a man named Jairus, a ruler of the synagogue, came and fell at Jesus' feet, pleading with him to come to his house 42 because his only daughter, a girl of about twelve, was dying. As Jesus was on his way, the crowds almost crushed him.
49. While Jesus was still speaking, someone came from the house of Jairus, the synagogue ruler. "Your daughter is dead," he said. "Don't bother the teacher any more."
50. Hearing this, Jesus said to Jairus, "Don't be afraid; just believe, and she will be healed."
51. When he arrived at the house of Jairus, he did not let anyone go in with him except Peter, John and James, and the child's father and mother.
52. Meanwhile, all the people were wailing and mourning for her. "Stop wailing," Jesus said. "She is not dead but asleep."
53. They laughed at him, knowing that she was dead.
54. But he took her by the hand and said, "My child, get up!"
55. Her spirit returned, and at once she stood up. Then Jesus told them to give her something to eat.

WHICH MIRACLES?

Throughout these accounts Jesus displays more emotion than elsewhere. This is most famous when he cries during the story of the raising of Lazarus. One could search for profound reasons for this but the common sense explanation is probably best. Bereavement is a highly emotional time and the emotions of relatives and anyone else surrounding the death is heightened to an extent that was unlikely to leave Jesus untouched. It also is a stark reminder that death brings with it very strong social emotions which are indeed part of the process of dealing with the death and which go through their own stages which in some way punctuate the stages of mourning. Each act surrounding the deceased demands a different emotion suited to the physical task which must be conducted – be it laying out the body, attending the funeral or tending the tomb as Mary did that of Jesus.

The miracles performed by Jesus usually caused controversy. First, Jesus was accused of breaking the Sabbath by healing a man's withered hand. (Mark 3:1–6) Jesus defended his right to heal on the Sabbath by posing the question, "Which is lawful on the Sabbath: to do good or to do evil, to save life or to kill?" (Verse 3) Second, illness was often thought to be the consequence of an individual's sin or that of his parents. Jesus provoked the anger of 'some teachers of the law' when he forgave the supposed sins of a paralysed man lowered through the roof.

> "Why are you thinking these things? Which is easier: to say to the paralytic, 'Your sins are forgiven,' or to say, 'Get up, take your mat and walk'? (Mark 2:8b and 9)

Now, the miracles in which Jesus raised the dead did not result in such controversies with the notable exception of Lazarus. Was it because death is universal and blameless in all but a minority of instances? Dead bodies were certainly unclean and prescribed rituals overcame these problems. Jesus did not seem to violate these or cause any offence. Nevertheless, Jesus did incur the ridicule of the mourners as in Mark 5, verse 40a.

29

They probably resented Jesus' intrusion into their mindset of deep grief. However, their grief soon turned to adulation.

Two further points must be noted. These miracles were essentially private affairs, no more so than in the raising of Lazarus. Jesus travelled with only his most trusted disciples and carried out the miracle in seclusion and quietness. He further instructed the families and other witnesses to keep quiet about the outcome. Last, when Jesus healed the sick, he often used an argumentative formula or a teaching rhetoric but in these miracles (with the exception of the raising of Lazarus) there was no such debate. He did comment on the faith of Jairus but not at the time of the miracle.

As stated above, the miracle of the raising of Lazarus will neither be printed nor dealt with here. The miracles of the synoptic gospels are cleverly worked narratives which contain profound truths, whereas John does not stop at simply giving us carefully worked narratives but offers theology, usually through the words of Jesus. These words are so important that they deserve a chapter to themselves.

However, the next chapter speculates on the nature of the mortal body which the recipient of life may have had after its restoration. All the miracles fail to offer any guidance or clues on this vitally important and fascinating issue.

Chapter III

Our Mortal Bodies and Immortal Souls

It is an abiding mystery of the miracles which have just been discussed that we know almost nothing about the subsequent life of those who are raised from the dead. One very simple explanation may be that none of them are named except by their first names and their families are hard to identify. The families of Lazarus and that of Jairus might be identified but no record of the latter has come to my attention. What did the young persons do with the rest of their lives? We can speculate as to what kind of life they led; was it good, bad or utterly carefree? As in so many of the healing miracles, we have no record of what happened to those who were healed.

Those who were raised like us had bodies to be cherished. They must be nurtured as the vessels which will carry our souls through life, unto death and God's final judgement. Jesus' teaching in Matthew 25: 31–46 tells us quite plainly that the goats will be separated the sheep that will enjoy the Master's pleasure. Those so chosen had pursued lives in unwitting righteousness in the service of others.

More troubling is the question of what Jesus and the other prophets and apostles actually offered these people who were returned to life. Had they been offered immortality or condemned to wandering the earth in some ageless form? If Dylan Thomas in his poem, *A Refusal to Mourn the Death, by Fire, of a Child in London*, is correct, '[a]fter the first death, there is no other'. (Thomas, 1974) Yet these people were subject now to the paradox of living mortal lives having been spared from mortality, early mortality, by God. They had to die of old age or of an accident, further illness or through conflict. Like people who have near death experiences, they were destined to taste death twice. If they were to live forever, it would be similar to Doctor Faustus' pact with the devil who gave up the opportunity of heaven for the earthly pleasures of carnal love and enjoyment. They too could do anything – actual historical Dr Who's. Likewise, those who were raised from the dead may have thought that they were absolved of all responsibility if they were to live forever. The only sensible answer is that they assumed a mortal frame, a body which would someday succumb to death.

They were not saved by Jesus; they were brought back to life. Salvation was to be earned in what remained of their earthly existence and to achieve this they had to follow Jesus. It is entirely probable that some of them had not acknowledged him prior to their illness and death but now had the choice – to follow or to carry on regardless.

I want to argue that they had been returned to mortal bodies similar to yours and mine and that they had to make the same journey to seek salvation by following Jesus, in order to inherit the immortality bought by him on the cross.

Ochs argues that prior to Jesus the people of the Old Testament followed a communal salvation. The Israelites knew the boundaries between displeasing God and living righteous lives which led to the building up of a nation of God's people pleasing in his sight. In the New Testament and indeed to this present day, Christians embark on a personal journey towards salvation and that salvation is sealed in their immortality at the time of their death. Ochs argues that all our actions in life have to be centred towards building a relationship with Christ in faith which leads to our salvation.

I have held the view that a good and loving God must offer us immortality as part of salvation. If God loved us by creating us it would be totally wrong to assume that he is going to abandon us at the time of our death. One second he loves; the next we are abandoned. Such a scenario is unthinkable. Jerry Walls puts the argument much more eloquently than I can.

> Here then is the connection between God's goodness and heaven. If God is perfectly good as well as supremely powerful, then he surely has both the ability and the desire not only to make himself known to us but also to preserve and perfect his relationship with us, if we are willing. A good God would not create us with the kind of aspirations we have and then leave those aspirations unsatisfied. If immortality is possible ... then it should also be judged to be probable, if God is good. (Walls, 2002; p 31)

Heaven is a measure of God's goodness and is offered to anyone who adopts the calling of a Christian. Many people assume that God's goodness is unlimited and available to all no matter what they believe. Such is the understanding of universalism. Such has been my own position for years but as I ponder I realise that such a position does not encourage any kind of commitment to Jesus or to the imitation of his life which is so vital to salvation. A blanket assumption that Jesus has purchased all our resurrections is a barren belief if it is not accompanied by the service of following him. As John Milburn, who is quoted by Walls, puts it, 'Death in its unmitigated reality permits the ethical, while the notion of resurrection contaminates it with self-interest'. (1999; p 34)

So what is the ethical? Salvation cannot be sought without a constant striving to act morally as Jesus would have. In John's gospel Jesus says, 'Greater love has no one than this that he lay down his life for his friends'. (John 15:13) The ethic of altruism is undergirded by our certainty of Christian immortality. It makes no sense to hope that our actions in the name of Christ are meaningful if there is no hope in the future. Self-sacrifice is good but ultimately meaningless if we have no understanding of heaven. Such a moral philosophy has been with us through many philosophers and was sealed in the arguments of Kant.

> A truly robust moral faith requires both belief in a moral orderer and a reasonable hope for deep and lasting happiness. In other words, moral faith is best sustained by a worldview that includes a doctrine of heaven. (Walls, 2002; p 167)

A Christian bases his morality on the teaching of Jesus which had behind it his faith and trust in his Father. Our actions in this earth are given meaning by our belief in the future life. We do not dictate a heaven of our own making. It is not some magical kingdom where we are reunited with all that we have lost in this life and given the opportunity of carrying on as before. It is where God's goodness meets our striving to please our master Jesus Christ. God determines heaven's nature not us. If we think otherwise, we are creating our own immortality independently of God and of any journey which he demands our life on earth should take.

It is thus the case that those who were raised from the dead had to pick up their lives and make the same decisions as we have to make about the nature of their journey and their way forward. So what is the nature of the body which carries the spirit which inspires us?

On death the body is little more than a heap of flesh, sinews and bones. But in life they are inhabited by the personality and vibrancy which the mind generates. Our souls give us the opportunity to respond to matters spiritual, to find God, and glimpse the immortality which may be ours in Christ. The individual must be treated and approached as a complete entity. Descartes placed all his emphasis on the mind and its ability to think. *Cogito, ergo sum*, diminished the body and matter to dualistic objects of investigation and instigated the long-held belief that the body was little else than an intricately designed machine which had to be maintained and repaired. Most would entertain the 'trinity' of body, mind, (or soul) and spirit as being the three most important aspects of a 'whole person'. More secular theorists tend to remain content with body and mind, *psyche* and *soma*.

It is these bodies which those who were brought back to life inhabited and with which they faced the same challenges as we do.

The body, or remains, are valuable to relatives and this is witnessed by the care and the love which goes into the funeral arrangements. My cousin told me of a very moving type of ritual in the poorest area of Somalia. Mothers would leave their families to take a child to the hospital run by *Médecins Sans Frontières* and when they were struck by serious illness. Often the children died but tradition dictated that the child be buried quickly in a very ornate cloth which was far beyond the resources of the mother. Yet between the nursing staff and the other patients money was always found to pay for such cloth. Plenty was conjured out of nothing. Modern funerals are no less elaborate in the West and undertakers have even broken into the television advertising market in ways which would have been taboo twenty years ago.

Early Christians similarly had to work out how they were going to value the remains of a dear one. A belief very quickly developed about the resurrection of the dead and people looked towards the final resurrection when the world would be consumed at the second coming. Tertullian wrote at some length about the resurrection. He lived between roughly 160 and 220 CE and was thought to be a lawyer writing in Latin. He defended the resurrection against the criticisms of heretics and other religions. More than anything surrounding the resurrection, he stressed the value of the body. From the remains, a new and incorruptible body could be raised and arguably he sets forth the argument for burial which ensured that the body remained for the time of resurrection.

Rather contrary to the ideas being presented here, Tertullian used the example of the resurrection of Lazarus to illustrate the process of the final resurrection. He argues that Lazarus' body was already corrupted and that Jesus overcame this in his miracle, just as Paul assured the early church of the resurrection in 1 Corinthians 15: 42–43 and that as the body which is 'sown is perishable, it is raised imperishable'. The problem that I have with this argument is that the resurrected Lazarus was still mortal in spite of the miracle. The argument of Tertullian runs in his book, *On the Resurrection of the Flesh*, thus:

> Now in the case of Lazarus, (which we may take as) the primary instance of a resurrection, the flesh lay prostrate in weakness, the flesh was almost putrid in the dishonour of its decay, the flesh stank in corruption, and yet it was as flesh that Lazarus rose again— with his soul, no doubt. But that soul was incorrupt; nobody had wrapped it in its linen swathes; nobody had deposited it in a grave; nobody had yet perceived it stink; nobody for four days had seen it sown. (Chapter 53)

However, there is a wider problem which had to be addressed by the early apologists. There was a wide spread belief that the soul was immortal. At first sight Christians would agree with this but the uniqueness of their belief was that the soul maintains all of the identity which goes with everyone to their death.

It remains in God's care and under his judgement. The soul has no other life or a new identity in a fresh body with a good or bad karma. The Christian's journey has ended unlike the endless wanderings of other religions. God's unique concern saved souls which have been carried by our frail bodies through the trials of our earthly sojourn. Without an identity built up during our mortal existence there would be no settled immortal future stretching into eternity. Without individual divine judgement, there would be no crown of victory, nor eternal damnation for others. Those who were raised in scriptural miracles were expected to participate in the same spiritual strivings as we are today.

> Blessed is the man who perseveres under trial, because when he has stood the test, he will receive the crown of life that God has promised to those who love him. (James 1: 12)

Minucius Felix argued strongly against any suggestion that only the soul survived. He was aware that all sects who believe in the immortality of the soul could also believe in reincarnation or at least the idea that the soul could be born with a new identity in another animal. He firmly maintained that the Christian soul's identity was guaranteed by its inherent link to the body. Resurrection for a Christian was resurrection of the body and thus the immortal soul would maintain its individual identity at the last day. Only thus could there be any form of judgement between those welcomed into God's nearer presence and those condemned to eternal damnation.

Minucius Felix was not as concerned as Tertullian about the disposal of the corpse. He recognised that bodies could be lost in fire or drowned at sea but he contended that God was always able to unite the body with the soul. If God had the power to create mankind out of nothing, surely he had the power to resurrect the body and soul from whatever state thus ensuring the individuality of the soul:

> Do you think that, if anything is withdrawn from our feeble eyes, it perishes to God? Every body, whether it is dried up into dust, or is dissolved into moisture, or is compressed into ashes, or is attenuated into smoke, is withdrawn from us, but it is reserved for God in the custody of the elements. (*Octavius*, Chapter XXXIV)

It was only in 1884 that cremation was decriminalised in the UK and the first crematorium was founded in Woking in 1878. It was first used in 1886. Even then it was a requirement that the ashes (a misnomer for the remainder of the bones) be buried in an identifiable grave in the grounds of the crematorium. I believe that Minucius Felix opened the way to cremation at a very early stage of development of Christian doctrine which was not recognised for much more than a millennium and is now accepted by many denominations in many countries.

... ...

As for man, his days are like grass,
he flourishes like a flower of the field;
the wind blows over it and it is gone,
and its place remembers it no more.
Psalm 103: 15 & 16

Tenderly he shields and spares us;
Well our feeble frame he knows.
In his hands he gently bears us,
Rescues us from all our foes.
Henry Francis Lyte

Frailty may manifest itself in at least three ways. First, in ageing; second, illness takes its toll; and third, the exigencies of our earthly existence take their toll.

The frailty of our bodies is the strongest indicator of our ageing and is also the greatest threat to our well-being. Our bodies suffer from wear and tear and we almost all learn to grow old gracefully. Most people accept that with old age comes infirmity and we all expect to go to hospital sometime to have surgery to repair some weakness or faulty organ. This of course is new; the surgery of today prolongs life far beyond the dreams of previous generations and with more skilful care risk has been diminished.

Job did not suffer from the hardships of natural disaster but rather from bodily afflictions which were visited upon him. Natural disasters underline our frailty in another way – we cannot protect ourselves from the misfortunes which the world may bring. Job suffered on his own which was why he was so afflicted by illness. It is worth remembering, however, that although the flesh may suffer our spirits are much more robust, as was Job's. He withstood his trials not because of the strength of his body but of his spirit.

Illness can be a very draining experience and it is the strength of the spirit which inspires others to admire those who prevail against modern cancers and acquired disabilities. It, and for that matter frailty, has been described as somewhat like a serial progression of health problems. (Kleinman, 1988; p 232) Old people make up a substantial percentage of disabled people and do not in fact regard themselves as being disabled. Disabling conditions like Alzheimer's, arthritis and the after effects of a stroke are often seen as inevitable diseases of old age. Without the strength of spirit our lives would be a downward spiral of suffering but the spirit which was tested in Job, and since has been tested millions of times, mitigates the frailty which is built into all our lives.

The third measure of frailty is mankind's predisposition to sin and the consequences which are either inflicted by others or self-inflicted. This has been a constant theme in the epistles of Saint Paul and throughout Christian literature.

St Paul captured the human predicament excellently in his letter to the Romans. He had no doubt that men and women had a capacity to do good but was aware that more often than not we are alienated from ourselves and do not achieve the good that we would do. The condition of fallen man is that he cannot achieve good every time by his own devices. This is the essence of faith versus works. Works represents the good that we would all like to do but our deeds cannot come to full fruition without faith. Faith resides in the spirit which can only be found if a decision is made for Christ and by our attention to the Spirit, faith may bring about good in our intentions towards others and the world. Paul wrote:

18. I know that nothing good lives in me, that is, in my sinful nature. For I have the desire to do what is good, but I cannot carry it out.
19. For what I do is not the good I want to do; no, the evil I do not want to do—this I keep on doing. (Romans 7: 18 and 19)

What Paul highlights is the struggle which all human beings have in following Jesus and doing his will in such a way that good may be achieved. The most unfortunate thing in the human predicament is that we know some of our failings and we know how they can be thwarted by the weakness of our flesh even though the spirit is willing. Our failures mount up and our frailty can only be relieved by seeking forgiveness for the ways we have gone wrong. This is the inherent frailty of men and women but our consciousness leads us to strive to do what we know to be good. The striving is both the pain and the thrill of faith and without it our alienation becomes our despondency and wandering from the path of God. There have been many secular versions of alienation which have inspired generations but have never held the truth which was spelt out by Paul. Marxist projects were amongst the most idealistic in the world but they failed because of our inability to carry them through. Without the backing of faith, many of the projects lacked moral conviction even although many sought to deliver good. The journey Paul set us was more realistic in that it has at its heart the human condition of striving to please God but failing because of the nature of our shortcomings. Life is seen as a pilgrimage and we face the hurdles which are placed before us in our endeavours to imitate Christ. *The Pilgrim's Progress* by John Bunyan is the classic example of such literature written in the late seventeenth century. The pilgrim is tested by the evils of the world and his own moods such as despondency, and at the last comes through to ultimate victory. He has faced up to 'hobgoblins' and 'foul fiends' and survived the many mires of his own making to reach the celestial city.

Hobgoblins are not weird, wizen creatures but rather the obstacles, seen and unseen, which drag us away from the good of the pilgrimages in the name of Christ. What Bunyan does in his book is build up a series of examples of the obstacles which the Christian pilgrim must face, and shows how many fall by the wayside as their spirits weaken and fail to live up to the faith which is exemplified in the life of the Christian pilgrim allegorised in the story.

Modern curses such as excessive alcoholic consumption, illegal drugs or smoking bring their own frailties on increasingly young bodies, both male and female, and result in suffering which whilst for a few may strengthen faith in adversity or in many cases drive one away completely to sulk and be angry with God. The world, in short, is a dangerous place beset by illness, violence and warfare which do little to afford our bodies the security of growing old, not only gracefully, but in grace. At the end, it is the gracious who can confidently face God. However, many others have been overwhelmed by the temptations and trials of this world.

Connected of course to this third kind of frailty is the inability of many to find any faith even in the so called Christian society. The need for a decision in favour of Christ is jut as great today as it was when Jesus walked the earth.

The problem of evil has long occupied theologians and what follows is the most optimistic solution. Irenaeus drew upon the biblical formula that God made man in his image and likeness and argued that whilst we are all born in his image we learn through religious devotion to grow into his likeness. Hick (1966) adapted this patristic model to develop the notion that we all live this life in a 'vale of soul-making' where we are gradually brought through our experience and suffering to a greater likeness of God. There was a virtue in suffering which brought with it the reward of a closer likeness to God, reassured by the fact that we have witnessed God's own suffering in the death of his son on the cross.

Those who were raised from the dead entered the rest of their lives threatened by the same frailty but with a strengthened spirit, which we can only hope was present as it is never mentioned in the Gospels.

There is little doubt that fallen man is weak. Mankind has tasted death since the fall and has failed to overcome it. The only record of such victory lies in the resurrection of Jesus Christ. Jesus performed many miracles in his ministry but never once demanded anything in return. He was impressed by people's faith and by the closeness of God to those who were rescued from the stigma of illness or the sting of death but thereafter they enjoyed the freewill to follow Jesus or not. I have said, not for the first time, that we do not know how their lives developed. However, what we do know is that their lives remained mortal and their pilgrimages began from the moment of their cure. If they attempted to overcome the frailties of their existence and understood the imperative of following Jesus there is a chance that they would eventually achieve the crown of glory. From their encounter with Jesus, they would discover what God values in life and that is the subject of the next chapter. Our Christian experience and faith helps us to build inner strength and fellowship in Christ and in human love, to help face the trials and vicissitudes of our final years, months or days.

Chapter IV

Core Values of Life

God reveals himself in all his miracles but in the case of those we are examining, he reveals some of the values which are necessary to make life fruitful and worth living. These values do not presuppose belief in all cases but are greatly enhanced by a searching faith for salvation in Jesus Christ. God offers life, not just in terms of vital signs, but in all its fullness of lives lived in the comforts of his providence. What this chapter does is to identify some of these values and place them in the context of human contentment and happiness. Because God is content to offer qualitative life to everybody, these values are universal but to reject them is to endanger one's place in the order of the kingdom of God proclaimed by Jesus.

Our faith is peopled by many values. Most come in God's commandments and in the golden rule of Jesus but others can be gleaned from our interpretation of scriptural stories. Markham argues that such values tend to come in families and are representative of such things as combating poverty, family values and personal values of life. In modern society these values often conflict with other religions and, in particular, with secular society and concomitant legislation. The church has learnt to compromise with majority opinion, which it has done so with the loss of status and it own confidence about how far it should stand up for its own values. Markham examines the limits of tolerance and how far the church should accommodate other views. He argues quite conservatively that we must stand firm on many of our values and understand their goodness. To proclaim them is to broadcast the gospel. Assisted death was discussed in an earlier chapter and can be cited here as one example where the church may take a stance, but the miracles we are discussing throw up other values which are important and require decisions as to the limits of tolerance.

Some of these values fit conveniently into the families to which Markham alludes. (Markham, 1999) Thus, we find that we must comment on poverty when we read the stories of Elisha and Elijah. Compassion is another such value and can be seen in all the miracles under discussion and lastly the Bible clearly celebrates family bonds and the social setting of life. And so to move to poverty.

Poverty

It is often argued that Jesus had a 'bias towards the poor'. It is further argued that because Jesus was born in humble circumstances that God demonstrates his bias in every aspect of his son's life. This argument has always been suspect: God's love is not just for the poor but for all and his salvation is offered in equal measure to all. God 'causes his sun to rise on the evil and the good, and sends rain on the righteous and the unrighteous' (Matthew 5: 45), and we forget this at our peril. Similarly, Jesus said, 'the poor you will always have with you'. This is not a license to live regardless of the poor but simply to recognize that no matter how much poverty is eliminated, there will always be someone poorer than others (Matthew 26: 11). What Jesus does show is obedience to what George Newlands calls 'the compassionate imperative' which demands that we respond to the poverty and suffering which is around us. The 'Make Poverty History' was mistaken in its blatant optimism yet it responded to the commands of Christ to care for the poorest and to end the worst manifestation of poverty.

> We may look at life, death and resurrection from the perspective of Jesus as a person. We may also reconsider the Christological centre from the perspective of the traditional doctrines of atonement and reconciliation. Of course, for the Christian faith what Jesus achieves as reconciler derives from his simply being who he is. His presence, then, in a particular context and now universally has a transformative influence on faith just by being there. Human lives are deeply influenced by the presence of others. There presence is

cashed out in their actions, in sympathy, in actions of kindness and effective intervention on behalf of others ...
(Newlands, 2006; p 85)

Newlands points out that all lives are influenced by the presence of others. Jesus also showed an interest in his heavenly father's value of man as a social animal as part of a family and of working relationships within and beyond that family. Thus Jesus demonstrates that God values all that tends towards our welfare. Work, mainly agricultural work in the Bible, adds to the wellbeing of mankind as does work within the context of the family. Jesus also shows a profound respect for the emotional bonds which are formed by kinship and friendship and demonstrates that compassion cannot be offered and experienced without emotional involvement. All these strands must now be unravelled in an examination of miracles under study.

First, let us return to poverty in these miracles. In almost every case of our resuscitation miracles, there is an awareness of the loss of a valuable contribution to that life's gathering of the means to live. In the Old Testament, both the miracles of Elijah and Elisha took place in the midst of severe poverty. Famine was either stalking the land or was about to and the Israelites were deeply distressed by the plight in which they found themselves. 2 Kings has tragic images of Elisha's involvement with those afflicted by hunger and famine. At times it seems as if the gospels almost mirror his ability to spread food over a large number of people. Such a story occurs in 2 Kings 4: 42–44 where Elisha assures those around him that a meagre supply of bread would feed a hundred men in much the same way as Jesus fed five thousand with five loaves and two fishes. The wisdom of kings is also brought into question as they have to tussle with hunger during a siege when mothers have a choice between living and sacrificing their children or perishing altogether. There are stories of how the law is used to address poverty. Elisha encourages the Shunammite widow to flee with her revivified son for seven years to escape famine. On her return her property has been appropriated and the compassion of the king is illustrated by his concern that her property should be returned to her after examination by an official. The compassion, for a second time in the son's life is a sign of God's concern for their wellbeing and the good of those who suffer both from famine and injustice (2 Kings 8: 1–6) Elijah demonstrated his miraculous ending of poverty by eking out the small supplies which were available to the widow of Shunem. But despite his seeming holiness and goodness, he failed to protect the widow from the worse fate – the death of her son. Such a death showed the poverty of her belief and also the extent to which people counted upon the extended family to act as an economic unit in the production of food.

Amidst the famine of 2 Kings there is obviously the fingerprint of God's compassion acting through the hearts of those in authority. It is not new to Kings but can be found in the compassion of Joseph in responding to his family's needs at the time of their famine. Compassion serves as an illustration of God's will and guidance in the work of salvation which demands compassionate hearts. The case of the Shunammite woman illustrates this well. By God's compassion and power, the son is raised from the dead and given new life but is offered it more abundantly when he is protected from the ravages of poverty by the compassionate king who restores his mother's property. Jesus the good shepherd said, 'I have come that they may have life, and have it to the full'. (John 10: 10) The good shepherd seeks to preserve the lives of his sheep. Here we have such a saying prefigured in the life of this boy. Life is important to God.

Jesus was not ashamed to talk about the economics of life in his parables. His parables covered the very poor and the wealthy but in every case he used the story to illustrate devotion and duty to God as revealed through his word in the parables. Jesus spoke of the widow's mite – the very smallest amount a poor person could offer to the treasury. (Mark 12: 41–44) He also spoke of the consequences for the rich of neglecting the poor when he described the torments of the rich man in Hades who ignored the plight of Lazarus the beggar at his gate. (Luke 16: 19–31)

Many of his parables were set in an agricultural context. Even the story of the prodigal son is a rural story about a farmer and his son who sinks to the lowest of the low as a swine herd. When he speaks of the rich in his parables, he does so to illustrate how the riches of his word should be employed to bring maximum glory to God. Such is the story of the talents in its various forms. Jesus had a profound awareness that life in Palestine took place in the context of agriculture and the struggle to make the most of the gifts which God gave to enable life.

It is exactly the same with his miracles. Each of the people who had died either carried the hopes of their families or already contributed to the welfare of their close knit groups. In restoring life Jesus knew that he was giving back the opportunity to be part of the struggle to produce goods that were important to those who were bereaved. In the Acts of the Apostles, there is an awareness that those whose lives were lost were significantly involved in the struggle to survive. Even Tabitha, as a missionary, produced material goods which helped to sustain life.

Collective Faith

Death invariably brings a crisis of faith with it. Such crises are not always negative. As faith may be weakened; so it may be strengthened. The experience of bereavement usually prompts some thinking about the meaning of life and its values. Until very recently most people professed some kind of faith because the church, particularly the established churches, were the only bodies which offered expertise in conducting funerals. The cultural scene has now changed greatly with humanist funerals and those of other faiths. However, there must always be a decision to trust someone to conduct a ceremony which will bring closure to the deceased life. We can only approach a practitioner whom we trust and that may prompt an examination of faith. Alas, for many there is a negative reaction to Christian faith and others are asked to perform the ceremony. In each of the miracles under review, someone was asked to help or someone was rejected. Such is the nature of the crisis of faith which occurred in these miracles.

I have doubts about the value of constantly stressing faith as the prime mover in miracles of any kind in the New Testament. It is a narrow understanding of the miracles to only regard them as the vehicles of expressing faith in Jesus. They manifestly have many other properties which are of equal or even more importance. The idea of preaching constantly about miracles as either exemplars of faith or the power of God is to miss some of the wonders of the miracles. (See Monteith, 2005; chapter 3)

Faith can be a great motivator and anyone who has conducted a funeral must know that a large amount of trust by the chief mourners must be vested in the minister. To lose it or betray it may have life-long adverse effects on relationships. Charisma can be added to trust in the cases of Jesus, Paul, Elijah and Elisha.

The predominant faith which is evidenced in the miracles is precisely of the type which all of us vest in someone at the time of bereavement. The miracle workers were very seldom 'on the scene' in the majority of the stories under discussion. In fact, a major part of the narrative of stories like that of the raising of Lazarus is the absence of Jesus. In other instances Jesus had to be sought and faith declared in him as part of a belief that he could rectify the situation. The same was true of Elijah and Elisha. Two different kinds of faith are illustrated. First, some relatives showed a deep faith in Jesus as a teacher, possibly at best a messiah. Second, there was a faith in Jesus' presence which could only be exercised by his physical arrival on the scene. In both cases, a true and deep faith in Jesus was shown by all those affected by the bereavement. In sum, his presence bestowed both calm and peace on a troubled situation and his actions had these very qualities compared to the normal behaviour of people who have been bereaved. All the characters showed a great calmness in a situation which was desperate to the onlooker but controlled to Elijah and Elisha, Paul and Jesus. This shows that a third kind of faith was present. Each had a faith that God would not let them down in a crisis and that he would resolve the situation no matter how far they had to travel or how far into the death process the deceased had travelled.

Family Values

19. When you are harvesting in your field and you overlook a sheaf, do not go back to get it. Leave it for the alien, the fatherless and the widow, so that the LORD your God may bless you in all the work of your hands.
20. When you beat the olives from your trees, do not go over the branches a second time. Leave what remains for the alien, the fatherless and the widow.
21. When you harvest the grapes in your vineyard, do not go over the vines again. Leave what remains for the alien, the fatherless and the widow.
22. Remember that you were slaves in Egypt. That is why I command you to do this.
(Deuteronomy 24: 19–22)

Deuteronomy 24 is a perfect enshrinement in the law of the status of widows. It is not only simply laid out but beautifully so. The widow is to be honoured in her likely poverty wherever she may be and whatever her status. Her status is mentioned in the same breath as the stranger or orphan. The law which was laid down could be observed by all who tilled the land and made it quite clear that what we have must be shared with those who are less fortunate. The law, of course, was often more complicated and the book of Ruth reads almost as an early modern novel about how the widow should be treated by her kinsman Boaz. In days when there was no provision of welfare the extended family was of great importance in protecting the welfare of widows and orphans in the event of their husbands' and fathers' deaths. The magnanimity of Boaz in accepting Ruth in such effusive terms was the lasting message of the story and is the part most quoted even today. Ruth's story of harvesting the remaining crops in the field graphically illustrates the out-working of the Deuteronomic law.

The widow was a yardstick by which justice could be measured. If the people of God forgot them, they forgot a fundamental building block in any justice in their midst. Biblical people did not live the individualistic lives we now live, where the single remaining parent too often ends up in a nursing or retirement home where the family can forget her. If the justice which the Bible sought was to be effective, the family had to be strong, with a bond which went beyond some notion of sentimental love to a recognition that the welfare of the family was economic as well, and held the family together in times of prosperity and of famine as we have seen in the Old Testament. The maintenance of the family as a central block in the structure of society was protected from the breakdown of everyday catastrophes by care provided for widows and orphans.

It can thus be seen that the respect offered to parents was a vital part of life and was written into the Decalogue itself. Such respect was demanded of all families and in the event of bereavement was extended to the dependent status of the widow and orphan.

We can delve a little deeper into the significance of the miracles which involved a widow and her son. It is simple to suggest that the son was a source of income and support to the widow and that her loss was going to have dire consequences for the life which she would now have to live. But the statutes of God take the story to another level. The law is always particularly concerned about a childless widow. One such person would have the effect of bringing to an end a family line. Such a line was of great importance to Israelite society and to God's concern for the family as a building block of society. The law contained provision that a brother-in-law or other responsible kinsman would take responsibility for marrying the widow and thus continuing the family line. This provision not only ensures that the family life line would be continued but offers a degree of welfare to the widow. If children existed there remained a chance that the family name would be continued and the widow would be cared for in later years, but none of this was true for the childless widow. This begins to show the great significance of the death of a child and also the strength of the miracle of reviving an only child. This is how an African writer sums up the situation of the widow of Nain:

> ... in Jewish tradition widows were part of the group known as *anawin* – the poor ones of Yahweh. She was not just a widow, she was poor; and losing her only son meant losing her lifeline, her support, her hope for the future, her connection to the community. Her grief is multi-faceted. Her poverty is deepened for she has nothing to live for.
> (Njoroge, 1997: p 427f)

Children were honoured by God and manifest signs showed this. The fact that Jesus called children to his side is not just a pretty picture but is an affirmation of God's concern for them. There is also the beautiful image, in the prophet Isaiah of children being able to play at peace in the streets of the city after the ravages of unrest and deprivation had passed. Such an image has resonance today when parents appear so hesitant to let their children play on their own, and society seems obsessed by paedophilia. God's general concern for the young in our midst is reflected in his concern for the children who were revived in the miracles.

There is a mistaken theory held by some who have a literal belief in these miracles that God chose to only raise the young and that we can only aspire to do likewise. Apart from its serious neglect of the elderly, such a theory does not look behind the miracles to the texts which clearly place children to the fore. Jesus had a concern for all the laws which protected widows and orphans and reinforced family values.

At a very basic level the concern for family values shines through these miracles. The deceased is always supported by family members who grieve in the way appropriate to biblical culture. They gathered round and showed the normal emotions which all of us will experience at some time. Occasionally, they were angry, if not at God, at least at the holy man or Jesus himself. They often went into 'auto-pilot' in that they knew what had to be done and got on with it. None of the deaths which we have dealt with were tragically alone or one where no one had any real cause to mourn but rather the opposite. The family and friends gathered round and there was no suggestion that the death was some isolated act without consequences for others. These were no suicides nor chosen deaths but lives taken at an untimely time of life, and with consequences which were regarded as wholly negative and without relief to the deceased. Each one was tragic in a different way and quite beyond the comprehension of the next of kin.

The two stories in the Acts of the Apostles of Eutychus and Tabitha illustrate the types of faiths mentioned above but also introduce us to another aspect of faith. Eutychus and Tabitha both belonged to households of faith. Eutychus was worshipping in the midst of local converts to Christianity, and Tabitha had been surrounded by those to whom she ministered and was now surrounded by them in death. Such households of faith illustrate that no one should be left alone to face death when there is a clear Christian call to worship in both the context of life and death. It has been suggested by some theologians that it is only in the context of worship that surprising things happen, and after a long night of worship the reviving of Eutychus was both surprising and a vivid illustration of the newness of life which comes from faith. Tabitha in her own way illustrates exactly the same situation. God did not desert those who strove to illustrate faith in the life of a community. The community to which Tabitha belonged was defined by faith and by the purpose of being the church in a new community. Being the church meant standing with those who suffered and those who died in the service of the new gospel which had to be spread.

We cannot live well-balanced lives without various *rites de passage*. Life is punctuated by births, weddings and funerals and all of these are most successful when they are conducted in an atmosphere of faith. Faith that a child will grow into a Christian; faith that a marriage partnership will be sustained by love and faith and faith in death that the deceased will receive the 'crown of glory' and that we who are left will emulate his or her faith in our own lives that remain to us. Christianity is not a religion of individuals and their egos but is the combined expression of fellowship and faith shown in the lives of people living in a communal life of faith. The individual who harbours a faith of their own which is shared with no one is contradicting all the traditions of faith that have been built up since the Old Testament right through to the New.

It is not possible to understand the Holy Spirit in isolation. The third person in the Trinity can only be revealed in the activities of the community of faith and we are called to be part of that. We are both in the workings of God and at the same time outwith it. This is the great insight of Barth and challenges us to accept that everything that happens in the church is part of the revelation of our knowledge of God and of his purpose. In the context of death this is no less true in that the promises of God can only be understood in our submission to his will and our recognition of what that purpose may be in the course of our lives.

The fact that on several occasions God willed that lives should be renewed by reviving those who had died is but part of the revelation of the workings of Jesus in the light of the spiritual values which will be brought by the comforter, the Holy Spirit.

The whole situation begs one final question. When God restored life, did he restore it simply as the restoration of all the vital signs or did he restore spiritual life as well? There was any number of magicians in the Middle East who were capable of creating the illusion of bringing people back to life. Some may have revived someone who had all the outward appearances of just having died. Yet Jesus did not conform to this category. He spoke of faith and in John's gospel of the resurrection and he offered comfort to grieving families. Most of his miracles were conducted in private and certainly were not great spectacular events. Jesus had eschewed such spectacular shows of power when he resisted the temptations of the devil in the wilderness. It is therefore highly likely that he offered to those to whom he revived a spiritual life on top of the restoration of vital signs. There came with the new life all the benefits of the Holy Spirit and the comforts of following his will in life.

Yet this almost undoes some of my previous argument. I have argued that the revived people had to choose salvation in order to enter fully into eternal life. What Jesus illustrates is that he offers to these people, and to all of us an opportunity to enjoy a full spiritual life and participation in the new humanity but he leaves us the choice of whether we accept it or not. Here, my argument is re-enforced that Jesus could only offer full life if we accept his teachings and the way of the cross in our journey through life.

Lastly, the gospel does not offer an assurance of physical life. It is doubtful if Jesus was interested in that without the awareness of partaking in the spiritual journey of all his followers. What we are going to look at in the next chapter is how John's gospel spells out the immediacy of the gospel. Whilst resurrecting Lazarus, Jesus greeted him back to life with one of his seven great sayings which began, 'I am'. Lazarus was only raised because Jesus could say, 'I am the resurrection and the life'. Not tomorrow, not in the past but Jesus represented the resurrection here and now.

Chapter V

'I am the Resurrection and the Life'

> [The raising of Lazarus] is both the most profound expression of
> the power of the Son of Man and also contains the most poignant
> portrayals of Jesus' humanity, in which Jesus is described as loving
> his friend (11:3, 5), being deeply troubled (11:33, 38), and weeping
> (11:35).
> (Kinlaw, 2005; p 150)

This chapter is about Lazarus. There are in fact two such
characters in John's gospel and both show in different ways the
significance of their name, *El?azar Eleazar* ("God (has)
helped"). This name dramatically describes both of them. One
Lazarus was a destitute beggar who suffered a terrible life
begging at the gate of a rich man Dives who ignored him
studiously. After death, Lazarus luxuriated in heaven rewarded
for all his unwarranted earthly torments whilst Dives rotted in
hell because of his neglect of the poor at his door-step. (Luke
16:19–31) The other Lazarus was helped by God in another
way. He was brought back to life and joy was restored to his
family who were all deeply loved friends of Jesus. When Jesus
offered help he did so in the name of God and risked the wrath
of people, whether it was because they found his story-telling
offensive or his miraculous powers threatening and
inexplicable.

The gospel according to St John is apart from the other three
gospels which are known as the synoptic gospels – seen
through the same eye – which share material and tell much the
same story about Jesus. St John tells the story in a much more
theological way with a greater emphasis on the teachings of
Jesus and about Jesus. It begins with a prologue, John 1: 1–14,
which is obviously not the words of Jesus but sets the gospel in
a cosmic setting. God's value of life is shown in the delicate way
God allows his humanity in Jesus to offer life to Lazarus at

both a human level and at a divine level. God's gift to a dead Lazarus is the gift of life in the sacrificial giving of his Son – the precursor of the new humanity bought on the cross and sealed by the resurrection.

All four gospels emphasise the authority and status of Jesus but express this in different ways. John's prologue clearly states that Jesus is the eternal word of God made flesh. The synoptic gospels talk of Jesus as the Son of God whilst Jesus takes the authority into his very words in John's gospel.

This may give the impression that John paints a very intellectualized life of Jesus but in fact it is full of emotion and little phrases in his interaction with others which show his real humanity and true concern for those whom he held dear – his mother and indeed Lazarus himself. It was in this story of the raising of Lazarus that we read the verse, 'Jesus wept' (John 11:35). These human touches add both to the mystery and the authenticity of this account of Jesus' life.

The raising of Lazarus constitutes the longest story in the New Testament of such a miracle and it suggests that Jesus was a close personal friend of Lazarus and his sisters Mary and Martha. Mary was the woman who had shown her deep devotion to Jesus by anointing his feet with costly nard and wiping them with her long, flowing hair. (John 12:3) Although the other miracles may suggest that the prophets, apostles or Jesus may have had strong affinities with the person who had died, there was no suggestion that there existed a deep personal relationship such as Jesus obvious love for Lazarus' family. As in other miracles of this type, Jesus in this case was accused of letting the family down by not being present when needed but in this case Jesus responded emotionally and with an intimate liking for the family.

The authority by which Jesus acted is differently portrayed in John than in the other three gospels but they all have the same intention of showing that the kingdom was nigh and that Jesus had power over its enemies.

The 'I am' sayings

The use of 'I am' by Jesus has many ramifications and nuances which all help to point to the authority of Jesus. The saying occurs in two different contexts in John's Gospel. Hurtado makes the point that we underestimate the impact of the sayings if we simply concentrate on the seven 'I am' sayings. It is equally important to begin by considering the times when Jesus uses the saying without a predicate. (Hurtado, 2005; p 370) This is most apparent in the story of Jesus walking on the water where it is reported that he said to his disciples, 'it is I'. (John 6: 20) The disciples were confused by this figure walking on the stormy waters of Lake Galilee on their way to Capernaum and must have been more confused when Jesus made such a bold claim about himself and stressed such authority, authority over the elements as well as a general authority which suggested near equality with God. Hurtado characterises it as a moment of epiphany for the disciples. (*ibid*, 371)

Both Hurtado and McGrath discuss chapter 8 of St John's gospel. It is characterised by the saying, 'I am the Light of the World …' but then goes on to describe the encounter Jesus had with a hostile crowd which was incensed by Jesus' description of his own identity. He begins modestly enough by attributing all authority to God:

48. The Jews answered him, "Aren't we right in saying that you are a Samaritan and demon-possessed?"
49. "I am not possessed by a demon," said Jesus, "but I honour my Father and you dishonour me.
50. I am not seeking glory for myself; but there is one who seeks it, and he is the judge.
51. I tell you the truth, if anyone keeps my word, he will never see death." (John 8: 48–51)

When pushed further Jesus used yet again the first person, at which stage the crowd take to stone him. By some strange route he manages to escape. The point is that they are objecting to his self-description which they regard as blasphemy despite the earlier verses which makes it clear that he is not assuming any authority other than that given by God.

58. "I tell you the truth," Jesus answered, "before Abraham was born, I am!"
59. At this, they picked up stones to stone him, but Jesus hid himself, slipping away from the temple grounds. (John 8: 58–59)

If Jesus had been stoned, the persecution and death of God's son would have been truncated into a few hours instead of the trial and the passion which befell Jesus at a later time.

The seven sayings could not have been authoritative without the insertion of 'I am' although it is difficult to rephrase them – 'The resurrection and the life are here and now' – may be a possible rendering. It is certainly didactic but lacks any authority or personality. This is not addressed to anyone in particular, but would simply be another wise saying. It is the kind of comment a theologian might make. But Jesus took ownership of these sayings and held them high as part of his mission or commission to do his Father's will. The early church wanted to worship Jesus and had to have the authority of 'I am' behind their Lord.

> As far as the Fourth Evangelist is concerned, the use of the divine name 'I am' by Jesus represents an appropriate expression of the Spirit or Word of God in and through the one with whom the Word/Spirit is now wholly at one: he can speak these words in a way that no other before him could. Nonetheless, presenting a human being as speaking these words not only on behalf of God and/or through the inspiration of God's Spirit, but as the Word become flesh ... (McGrath, 2001; p 114)

The ownership of these is not personal, as 'intellectual property' might be, but was earned by Jesus' obedience to his heavenly Father unto death upon the cross. McGrath argues that Jesus was following in a strong biblical tradition of using a term which first appeared in Isaiah, but he also makes the point that Jesus' use of 'I am' offered a much more profound understanding of how John understood Jesus. Jesus was 'the word made flesh' and this statement was boldly made at the beginning of the gospel; now it was to be seen in Jesus' teachings. The prologue to John's gospel is carried forward into these narratives and sayings. The seven sayings of Jesus in the first person illustrate his willingness to be identified with his father and be prepared to be persecuted for the audacity of his claim and nature of his ministry as both a teacher and healer.

It could be argued that by using this phrase, Jesus was setting himself up as another god. In other words, John was allowing the gospel to depart from the monotheism of the Jewish faith of which both he and Jesus were part. No such claim is justified, because Jesus stands to be judged as a sign of God's love which could only be revealed fully on the cross and in the resurrection. Jesus was not claiming divinity but referring to himself as one closely identified with God. Thus the sayings which he used taught in two ways. First, there was the content of the saying which usually referred back to the scriptures of the Old Testament and offered wisdom to those who could hear. Second, the sayings taught people about Jesus and his relationship to his father. They rejected his closeness to God as offensive and thus persecuted him, but the miracle of the resurrection finished the teaching for those who could see and who received the revelation of the resurrection either directly or indirectly by faith through the words of others.

> The Evangelist has thus developed the traditional Christian association between Jesus' obedience to death on a cross, and his subsequent exaltation and being given the name above all other names. The one who does these things had already become one with the Word, which is the Name, and it was this commissioning as God's agent which is demonstrated in his obedience to the Father, even to death on a cross. The exaltation then serves as a

further demonstration, as the agent indwelt by the name returns to heaven. (McGrath, 2001; p 112)

In sum, in this saying and in others we see Jesus working as his father would have him. There is a popular commentary by A M Hunter, published in 1968, which builds on the idea of Jesus as the faithful apprentice be it at the work bench with Joseph learning the crafts of carpentry or learning the will of God and the way in which he would operate to show his compassion to his people and to Lazarus in this particular instance. The faithful apprentice only acts as his master demonstrates. This book was written long before McGrath but suggests exactly the same thing that the quality which Jesus displayed above all others was obedience to his heavenly father and his desire not to do his own will but that of his father.

Another unique feature of this saying is that Jesus must be present. Lazarus could not be raised without him nor could a magician have stepped forward from the crowds that had gathered and performed the usual resuscitation miracle. It is the same when Jesus is teaching. In the case of the other six sayings, they could only be made in the presence of Jesus whose authority was greater than all previous teachers. The saying is referred through him to the people; it is not direct as other teachers would have done.

This brings us to the last sign of authority in John's decision to publicise Jesus' sayings in the first person. It comes as part of a long biblical tradition to emphasise that the words spoken are inspired words of God written by the hand of a prophet or evangelist in this instance. The tradition can be traced back to the revelation of the name of God to Moses in Exodus when he encounters God in the burning bush in the desert. 'I am who I am' declared Yahweh sealing for all time the name of God in the tradition of the Yahwehist writers. From this revelation stemmed all of Moses' power to speak to the Pharaoh and to the Israelites who were a motley band who had to be united by a diffident but powerful leader. From giving power to such a leader, the phrase was now used to emphasise the power of the words of the prophets who believed they were recording the words and thoughts of God in their oracles. Thus we have Isaiah 47:8 and Zephaniah 2:15 ("I am, and there is none besides me."). Both these verses, and others, project the strength of God's word by reminding the reader or hearer of the strength of the God who led the Israelites out of Egypt, smote many enemies and now spoke of the sometimes dreadful state in which Israel found itself.

> The Fourth Evangelist works within the context of the dynamic monotheism of first-century Judaism, and makes use of many areas of flexibility within that monotheism to present Jesus as God's legitimate agent, the one whom he sent, who carries out his will and bears his name, and who is thus worthy to be respected and obeyed even as one would respect and obey God himself. The 'I am' statements attributed to God in Deutero-Isaiah were spoken by the prophet, in the first person, on God's behalf. In later Jewish-Christian thought, the one who has now become incarnate as the human being Jesus is clearly considered to be the same one who previously spoke through the prophets. (*ibid.*, p 114)

It is therefore not surprising that John chose to do exactly the same to emphasise the authority of Jesus and to do so at precisely the points of his most important teachings. It represents a unique way of demonstrating who Jesus was and the power of his words whether they be linked to a miracle, as in this case, or to teaching at important moments of revelation. Finally, they represent the climax in the rising crescendo surrounding nature miracles such as walking on the water of the Sea of Galilee.

This more than anything shows John in a different light from the other evangelists. All of them were reporting the actions and words of Jesus but here we have a completed literary work uniting the prologue, the announcement that the word became flesh in Jesus, with the rest of his ministry and purpose. It indicates that the miracle of raising Lazarus could only have been done by Jesus and stood apart from all the other so called 'miracles' which were reported before and around the time of the ministry of Jesus. The saying, 'I am the resurrection and the life', forces us by its very structure to treat this miracle in a different and new way.

At Bethany

Twice, we have commented on the human side of John's gospel. There are many stories that make Jesus real and we must put this down to the inspired writing of John. The way in which he personalises Jesus begins in chapter 2 where we have the very touching image of Jesus' mother pushing him forward towards the miracle of changing water into wine, despite his reluctance to do such a miracle at such an early time and age. "My time has not yet come." (John 2:4) is one of many gentle ways of correcting the haste of his mother in a way similar to how many of us have experienced a pushy mum. The impatience of this story turns to care and pathos in the words of Jesus from the cross, where he shows great concern for his mother by ensuring that 'the disciple whom he loved' took care of her after his passion. These tiny remarks give humanity to Jesus, and are the opposite of the way Pasolini portrays Jesus as almost like a disembodied person striding around the Palestinian landscape in his film interpretation of St Matthew's gospel.

The story of Lazarus is full of such humanity. For a start, we know that Jesus is dealing with friends and who understands their ways and their habits. He knows that Martha busies herself around the house, whilst he can count on Mary's attention as he teaches. Their brother, Lazarus, is also a friend and may have been a follower. John carefully portrays the family, as indeed do the other evangelists in their account of such miracles, but he does so by concentrating on the almost mundane lives of Mary and Martha. Then we come to the climax of Jesus' humanity – he weeps as he did over Jerusalem and shows clear emotion for the loss of his friend. He is under pressure and criticism from the sisters for being late and failing to be around when he was needed. They must have known of his reputation for performing miracles but when it came to his friends, he let them down. Such was the portrayal of the personal dynamics of the sad situation which Jesus had encountered.

We have seen how scholars have shown how John makes it plain that Jesus was the Word made flesh and pre-existed with the Father. The humanity which John introduces underscores the other twin nature of Jesus. John's gospel can easily take on the Chalcedonian formula of the two natures of the Christ when we are compelled to consider the humanity which Jesus shows. (Hunsinger, 2000) When John talks of the logos, he is speaking of the divine nature of Jesus; in the glimpses into his humanity, John is showing that he was fully human. Barth writes of the humanism of God referring broadly to the disclosure of his humanity in the life of Jesus. (Barth, 1964/2003; chapter one) It was a real life not make pretend. Jesus suffers as a man in relation with others, just as he suffered in relation to his father when at prayer in the garden of Gethsemane. He held together the demands of divinity with the demands of humanity in his emotions and work. It was as if Jesus understood the duties of office and of station and held them together as an exemplar to us all.

The 'I' of 'I am' begins to take on body and the word does indeed show itself to have flesh. Jesus has grasped the moment and is ready to show his true nature in the miracle of raising Lazarus.

However, the story begins with a very problematic verse which can cause considerable heartache:

> Jesus said, "This sickness will not end in death. No, it is for God's glory so that God's Son may be glorified through it." (John 11:4)

Jesus made a similar remark when he healed the blind beggar in John chapter 9. Incidentally, this significant periscope is the setting for another 'I am' pronouncement, "While I am in the world, I am the light of the world." (John 9:5) There he seemed to suggest the fact that he would have an opportunity to cure the blindness which would bring glory to God:

> "Neither this man nor his parents sinned," said Jesus, "but this happened so that the work of God might be displayed in his life." (John 9: 3)

Lightfoot points out that the curing of blindness had long been prophesied in the Old Testament (for instance, Isaiah 53) and that Jesus was reflecting the reality of such times. (Lightfoot, 1956; p 190) It seems more fruitful to consider these remarks in the context of John's Christology which is consistently constructed throughout his gospel. It is important that we have a reasonable explanation for these remarks because they do suggest a conspiracy which portrays God in a cruel and manipulative way. Would God really cause blindness or the anguish of bereavement simply to glorify himself? If the answer is 'yes', our God is not one which I favour.

No, these remarks reflect a greater reality where the Son of God already has the power, but only reasonable power, to rectify the wrong which God so dislikes; namely suffering and deprivation. Lazarus would be raised in reasonable time when Jesus could reach his home in Judea, against the wishes of his disciples who thought that it was too dangerous to travel there.

When we consider the way in which Jesus was dealing with human beings as shown in John's gospel, there was an obvious unity between the presence of a great humanity combined with a previously unseen divinity which John consistently shows as 'the word made flesh'. Kinlaw shows how John's gospel has two major parts or themes prior to the passion narrative; the first theme deals with the way the word made flesh or the son of God deals with humanity; and the second theme shows how followers of Jesus are to behave and to be guided by that spirit. At no point was Lazarus neglected or uncared for by Jesus – our Lord chooses his time as circumstances permit.

> Repeatedly the divine identity of Jesus Christ had been demonstrated in the context of an abiding human identity. There can be no question of displacement of the human mind and there can be no signs of ecstatic behaviour.
> (Kinlaw, 2005; p 151)

Jesus does not solve problems as a magician nor does he entertain for the sake of attracting attention. Suffering cannot be avoided but it can be rectified and the fact that he waited until the fourth day after the death of Lazarus is not a sign of neglect but an avoidance of what Kinlaw calls 'ecstatic behaviour'. We forget at our peril the moral of the temptations which Jesus endured. (Matthew 4: 1–11) Tempted by the devil to do the spectacular, to be popular and to turn into a dictator, Jesus accepts a gentler and personally more risky way of serving humanity with which he identifies.

Jesus had to face several questions from Martha before actually doing anything to relieve their suffering. Within the story, there is a debate about the resurrection:

21. "Lord," Martha said to Jesus, "if you had been here, my brother would not have died.
22. But I know that even now God will give you whatever you ask."
23. Jesus said to her, "Your brother will rise again."
24. Martha answered, "I know he will rise again in the resurrection at the last day." (John 11: 21–24)

Time after time some preachers make the mistake of assuming that the miracles brought faith to the witnesses and beneficiaries. Very often they had faith. Such was the case with the father with an epileptic child who only needed to see the new depths of his faith in the light of Jesus' presence. Bultmann makes this point emphatically:

The closeness of God's reign puts enormous strains upon people's beliefs and Bultmann illustrates this with reference to the father of the epileptic boy in Mark 9:14–29. Of most concern in this context is verse 24:

> Immediately [after the cure] the father of the child cried out and said, 'I believe: help my unbelief!'

It is commonly assumed that the father believed and gained faith after witnessing the miracle, but Bultmann argues differently. More probably, the father did already believe in God and was well aware of his mighty works and providence. But he understood this as the work of a remote God. However in this miracle God had come near, so that now the father believed in God in a totally different way as one whose dawning reign extended to the humble care of his son. This interpretation offers a new richness to the text. Just as God is remote and near at the same time, so it is argued that he is also a God of the past, the present and the future. (Monteith, 2005; p 124)

The case is similar with Martha, and we must presume Mary, who are both well equipped to argue with Jesus over the nature of the resurrection of the dead. Martha shares a belief in the general resurrection at the end of time, when Jews believed that all righteous people would be raised, and the debate which she had with Jesus was perfectly in order and in fact illustrates that women were competent at that time to debate theologically. What Martha did not see was that in Jesus the 'here and now' had been achieved and that the Kingdom of God or the dawning of the end of time was already present. In this time Jesus represented the fulfilment of history and was offering the resurrection now not sometime in the future. Such was the glory to be revealed in Lazarus' death as Jesus stated on first hearing of his sickness.

In sum, John is at pains to make it clear in his gospel that Jesus was indeed 'the word made flesh' walking and talking on this

I AM THE RESURRECTION AND THE LIFE

earth. His very teaching shows us how to build a relationship with his heavenly father, our God, and his miracles show the value God places on life in its fullness in the case of the healing miracles, and in this case we can begin to unravel the values which God places as dear to himself in life.

We now move to the mechanics of the miracles but yet again we must place them in context. Many theologians and church fathers have written about the raising of Lazarus. It has to be said that most take an allegorical approach and see in Lazarus' rising from the dead a prefiguration, almost an illustration, of Christ's own resurrection. The mystery of Christ's resurrection is, to some, laid bare in the more graphic description of the victory over the decay that was now the state of the corpse of Lazarus. The whole family in fact is often used to lay bare Christ's resurrection. When Lazarus' sister Mary anointed Jesus' feet with oil at dinner six days after the miracle, it is often taken to be a preparatory act signalling the attempted anointing in the Garden of Gethsemane, but for Jesus such oil could have been kept for the day of his burial. (John 12:7) Thus he spoke with amazing perspicacity and resignation to his nearing fate. In the event, Nicodemus supplied ample oil after the Romans handed over the crucified body of Jesus. (John 19:39)

> Then Mary took about a pint of pure nard, an expensive perfume; she poured it on Jesus' feet and wiped his feet with her hair. And the house was filled with the fragrance of the perfume. (John 12:3)

And at verses 7 and 8:

> "It was intended that she should save this perfume for the day of my burial. You will always have the poor among you, but you will not always have me."

What Mary did on that occasion showed all the humanity which was in the love of the women who went to the garden on Easter Sunday. However, although the story of Lazarus helped to produce theology and proofs of the resurrection, it is not my purpose here to go into it. One mention must be made of proof – it is often argued that it is significant that God brought a corrupted, decaying body back to life in Lazarus and is evidence that he could do likewise in the case of the resurrection.

There are great similarities between the resurrection of Jesus and that of Lazarus but also considerable differences. First, it is important to note that both men were placed in tombs; they were not buried in graves dug out of the ground. This was a fairly common practice in Palestine and to some extent still is. Shrouds and grave cloths were used rather than coffins and the bodies were deposited in these cool cavities in the ground. Unlike many parts of the world today when burials involve a coffin and six feet of earth in an artificially dug grave, it is still the case in the Middle East that bodies are buried with great speed. The point about Jesus' burial was that it had to be done before the Sabbath and sunset. We in the modern west are used to long delays between death and burial as the demand for undertaking services and travel of relatives grows. To reveal the body meant the removal of stones rather than the gruesome exhumation we sometimes hear of today. The empty tomb of Jesus did not reveal a coffin broken asunder but neatly folded grave-clothes and the ability of Lazarus to remove his grave-clothes is an important feature in his story.

There are a few dissimilarities between the resurrection account and the raising of Lazarus. According to the gospel of Luke (24:1), the women visited Jesus' tomb, which had been provided by the wealthy Joseph of Arimathea, on the morning of the third day. Their purpose of the visit was to anoint his body. Was this a common custom? There is no such mention of this happening in any of the other stories. Easter day was the third day after Jesus' death – here, four days have elapsed since Lazarus died. Was his body anointed on the third day? I cannot tell. What is made clear about Lazarus' circumstances was that his body had begun to decay and smell. It is important that the gospel mentions this because it gives substance to the import of the miracle and heightens the tension felt by the family about Jesus' seeming neglect of their needs. The other important difference is that this rising from the dead takes place in the public gaze; the actual resurrection of Jesus took place without witnesses and only became public because news of the empty tomb spread, and then witnesses appeared to attest to his resurrection.

When Jesus called Lazarus out of the tomb, he did not enter it nor did he physically remove the grave-clothes. Lazarus emerged as the result of the words of Jesus. The word made flesh commanded nature without the intervention of physical means. At all points in the story we are reminded of the favoured status of Jesus with God.

> That Jesus did not go into the tomb to touch him or shake him awake or draw him out puts the resolve upon Lazarus himself. Jesus stood outside calling. And Lazarus responded, now double-bound by winding sheet and by the limits of the old life. He brought himself out, burdened with the fetid grave clothes he would need again and the feeble body which would die again. (Guthrie, 2005)

Jesus had achieved with his words that which none other could do with their magic. Earlier, Jesus had debated with Martha about the nature of the resurrection which she understood to be the last day and for the righteous of Israel; now she saw the resurrection in the here and now and had her beloved brother restored to her. But let us not forget the caveat of Suzanne Guthrie who makes the point immediately that Lazarus was going to have to die sometime. Once again, his salvation lay in the future, in his behaviour and beliefs and the strength of his faith in the future of an uncertain life. Jesus left this to him, he was not a dictator. What is certain is Lazarus was born into the reality of the resurrection which was secured by the action of God working through Jesus in the 'here and now'.

There are three ways in which God's value of the life of Lazarus is illustrated in this miracle. So far we have examined two of them. First, the humanity of Jesus stretched out to his friends in the time of their need. Second, St John makes it clear that Jesus held himself up as the servant of his father and carried within him the qualities of 'the word made flesh'. To do this was sufficient to bring about his downfall but to do it in the context of miracles which many could understand was to underline the point. At the centre of two of these miracles, there were 'I am' sayings which were incomprehensible to some and offensive to others. Third, we now move to the personal sacrifice of Jesus and to his disregard for the danger his words and actions put him in.

Suzanne Guthrie sums up the situation in which Jesus placed himself in the following passage from a sermon. It highlights all the points which remain to be made on the third issue.

> *By a cruel irony, Jesus will be put to death because he brought Lazarus back to life.* After the raising of Lazarus, the Sanhedrin gathers in that famous meeting where Caiaphas presents his troubling prophecy. Worried about the Roman occupiers and the attention drawn to Jesus by the people, they ask, "What are we to do? For this man performs many signs. If we let him go on thus, everyone will believe in him, and the Romans will come and destroy both our holy place and our nation." But one of them, Caiaphas, who was high priest that year, said to them, "You know nothing at all; you do not understand that it is expedient for you that one man should die for the people, and that the whole nation should not perish." So "from that day on they took counsel on how to put him to death" (John 11:47b-50, 53).
> (Guthrie, 2005)

Jesus had but a few weeks earlier escaped stoning in Judea when he dared to take unto himself the words 'I am'. His disciples were painfully aware of this and were keen that he should not enter that province again. But there was no way he could visit Lazarus' family without entering hostile territory once again. The territory was hostile to him and hostile in general so that both the Romans and the Sanhedrin were wary of anything that could disturb the fragile peace which existed between the two.

It is significant that in the other gospels the miracles which Jesus performed cause offence as in this case. However, in these gospels people objected to Jesus breaking their understanding of the Sabbath law. Whereas Jesus believed in works of mercy on the Sabbath, the Pharisees did not believe that healing was justified on any grounds. In this case, the raising of Lazarus had followed the curing of the blind beggar and Jesus' popularity, even among the Pharisees was growing and with it of course his teaching. Such a situation was dangerous in a volatile territory, so it is significant that the story of Lazarus prompted Caiaphas to call a meeting. Never had the persecution of Jesus been so closely linked to a miracle. The popularity was a threat – the population were to be kept calm and not stirred up by a new religious leader whose fame was spreading rapidly.

The ultimate sacrifice of Jesus was on the cross, but it is indeed an ironic twist to this miracle that it was achieved at the cost of such hostility from the Jewish authorities. It is as if Jesus' own sacrifice was tied up in the raising of Lazarus. His restoration to life was to become a major factor in the condemnation to death for Jesus. It could be interpreted as yet another twist in the allegory of the miracle which has been so loved as a method of exegesis by many commentators of all times.

Whatever Jesus did was done without consideration of the cost. His teaching was strong and its strength lay in his ability to match his authority to his instinctual feelings about his relationship with his heavenly father. His miracles, likewise, would have been as nothing had they not had the authority of God behind them. God revealed his son through them, not to demonstrate his power or greatness but to show how much he values the marginalised, the grieving and the lost ones who were to be gathered together by the good shepherd. God's value of life shines out through the confusions of this miracle, the confusion of a grieving family and the angry confusion of a Jewish nation trying to keep the peace between themselves and the Roman rulers.

There is a remaining uniqueness in the story of Lazarus which is worth singling out. There are very few miracles where we are told much about the subsequent life of the subject of a miracle. We hear of the tenth leper who returned to Jesus after being cleansed but we do not hear what happened to the other people who were brought back to life or given a new beginning in a society which was so intolerant of illness and deformity. However, there are accounts of the life of Lazarus well after Jesus' death on the cross and these should be mentioned with the caveat that none of the accounts may be true.

The account which I favour is that Lazarus became bishop of Larnaka and Kittim in Cyprus. Such a story would illustrate that Lazarus used the blessing of life well into old age in the service of God and his master Jesus. His ability to preach and to talk personally as a witness of Christ's ministry would have been invaluable in a country which was not too far away from Palestine and open to ready commerce with that country.

The other account unfortunately leads to the infamous *Da Vinci Code* which I find amusing but quite offensive as a serious thesis. Part of the history is recounted in a thirteenth-century book, *The Golden Legend*, which was a 'best seller' for its time as a compendium of stories about the saints. The legend has it that Lazarus along with his sisters, Martha and Mary travelled to Marseilles in France in a boat guided more by providence than skill. There they settled. The author actually spends more time telling us about Saint Martha than Mary, unlike Dan Brown. Martha lived a holy life near Avignon where she lived the life of a saint performing the mandatory but rather florid miracles required of her status. She lived as a vegan and fasted regularly every week. She was known for her holiness and simple life style. She abstained from sexual relations (de Voragine, 1260/1993; p 22f). What her brother did remains rather unclear but his presence is noted in the text and he clearly played a role in the family.

Neither story may be true, and the second one is certainly embellished by dragons and monsters but it is interesting to have some record of the life which was led after Jesus' influence in Lazarus' life.

These stories do remind us of our original theme that the people whom Jesus restored to life still had a life to lead and that that life could either be to the glory of God or frittered away as insignificant. In actual fact, doctors and nurses do report that people who have near death experiences are sometime traumatised for life and find it hard to cope. Death would have brought the promise of instant salvation to them all under the old dispensation of the Old Testament, but now their new life gave them a choice of living in Christ or choosing a path of perdition. Lazarus was the only instance of what might have happened.

C.S. Lewis writes in *A Grief Observed* of how he coped with the death of Helen, his wife whom he preferred to call H. in his book. In many parts of the book he laments her passing and his grief. In one such passage he is talking of the unbearable silence, the end of any conversation with the deceased contrasted with the peace which H. has and he cannot disturb. He suggests that bringing her back would be cruel and selfish and goes on to suggest that Lazarus rather than Stephen was the first martyr. As a question, he has no answer nor have I. It is good to think that Lazarus had the comfort of his family throughout his later life and perhaps we should leave it at that.

Chapter VI

Our Value of Life and Death

> By nature, people prefer total comprehension and control of the outer world, with the intent of serving ourselves. When we live with that notion, we cease being a symbol of what is potentially so special about human beings. We become our own idols with a disturbed sense of sovereignty, filling the world with selfishness, hypocrisy, callousness, terror, and even death. Where there is no acceptance of the ultimate authority, law, and goodness of God, any evil is permissible: "I think that if the devil doesn't exist, but man has created him, he has created him in his own image and likeness" (Fyodor M. Dostoevsky). (Schlessinger, 1989: 28)

The final two chapters are about the value we put on life in the 21st century. They are about the ascendancy of egotism and the decline of communal love. What or where is the role of religious belief? Is there room for the acceptance of God's value of life? There is a growth in the belief that we control our lives as individuals and that those around us are all secondary. In the background, the issues are one of euthanasia and assisted suicide but a bigger picture will be painted before we reach that point. This will be dealt in the next chapter.

The 20th century was a testimony to how little we value life. Mechanistic, industrial warfare took its toll in two world wars and countless other wars illustrated our inhumanity and willingness to put life at a lower level than political aims. This has continued into the first decade of this century and shows no sign of abating. Genocide reared its ugly head in the holocaust and has done so since in many other dreadful acts of atrocity in Africa and Asia. The way we watch television portrays violence that demeans us all in how much destruction of life can be entertainment albeit in fictional settings of crime. Not infrequently such episodes are copied in real life horrific crimes to which we seem to have no answer. Kate Berridge suggests that people's knowledge of real death has been supplanted by our all too intimate consumption of enacted violent death on television. (2001; p 246ff)

The churches have often been slow to defend life publicly with the singular exception of the Roman Catholic Church which often seems to be too extreme to be fully credible. The extremism of some fundamentalist American pro-life groups extends beyond the law. This raises an immediate issue. Life is valued because it is God-given, and throughout the development of scripture it has been defended and commandments have been laid down banning the killing that is so much glamorized in television. These arguments have been rehearsed frequently and the gift of life has been extolled as something God alone controls. 'Thou shalt not kill' is used to justify the preservation and protection of all life, but it is often done so unthinkingly without a great deal of thought being given to the skills and costs necessary to maintain life with a high quality of meaning. Scripture appears to ban abortion in ways which do not cover the complications which we have made today surrounding this issue, and the end of life has been complicated by medicine's ability to sustain life even when all meaningful interaction would appear to have left the poor victim of accidents or disease. One of the problems is that both pro-life and pro-abortion groups use different exegeses for the same proof-texts and the results get bandied to and fro. Thus the sixth commandment can either be read as prohibiting 'killing' or 'murder'. That, in turn, raises the issue of the exact moment life comes into being. Is it at the moment of conception or at some later significant stage in the embryonic development? It all boils down to each person's definition of life and the respect it is shown in the face of the many horrible dilemmas which pregnancy can place before women and parents.

The fear of death has grown despite the reassurances of scripture and for many the easiest way has been to opt out of life and any circle of love which might potentially be there to sustain life. The fear of pain, loss of dignity and control, and loneliness fill people with fear for their futures but as Keown says

> [It is] recommended that high-quality palliative care services should be made more widely available by improving public support for hospices, ensuring that all general practitioners and hospital doctors had access to specialist advice, and providing more support for relevant training at all levels. It also called for more research into new and improved methods of pain relief and symptom control. The enormous contribution made by the hospice movement shows what can be done, given sufficient commitment, skill, training and resources, to provide quality care for patients at the end of life. *There is no need for any dying person to experience unbearable suffering. The inadequate care that too many patients experience, even in wealthy, developed countries like the UK and the USA, is a shameful indictment of the shortcomings of society's attitude towards the sick and the dying. It is, however, an indictment of society's failure to provide adequate care, not society's prohibition of intentional killing.* (2002; p 277)

Thus, an argument from expediency is not going to be successful because society's shortcomings fail to offer a moral justification for euthanasia. Whilst people have fears about dying, as distinct from death itself, we must seek a reason why comfort seems to be unavailable and why fear may only be overcome in premature and voluntary death?

Much as the arguments about life being sacred may have great persuasive powers to encourage many to campaign for the preservation of life, I think there is another argument which can be offered. It probably has already been done so by many theologians but very often the argument is not taken to its logical conclusion. I am convinced that the battle to defend life will be lost as long as we live in an egotistical society and so we must look at how we can rein back such tendencies.

The chapter will be divided into roughly two parts: the first, is going to look at the philosophical route by which egotism has become so important and second, how this has pervaded popular culture and made autonomy over death so attractive to many, be it at the beginning of life or at its end. Throughout, what is now important is the perceived quality of life by the autonomous individual.

At the outset, I said that this chapter was about the rise of egotism and the decline of communal love. Both of these must be briefly defined. It would be good to be able to quote some empirical evidence that certain groups have not become atomised in our society. When I read certain books by authors like Reynolds, Swinton and Reinders, I felt that I was reading material which was quite right wing and illiberal, but gradually came to realise that they were describing a conservative reality which could help disabled people to live more comfortably in a society which condones elective abortions and euthanasia. It was only after hearing a lecture by Professor Paul Bloom that I began to realise that there was empirical evidence that religious groups tended to stand behind social issues which involved care and a concern for the value of life. Haidt (2007) has shown that people of a conservative inclination tend to look to social values more frequently than others. Those who are very liberal tend to have the attitude that if it does no one any harm then it should be permissible. Such an attitude would condone euthanasia and abortion, and this is borne out by experiments which show how liberals tolerate quite bizarre behaviour which conservatives with stronger social values might reject. Liberals were much more willing to tolerate incest than those who had stronger group values which might variously be described as conservative or traditional. Morality, according to researchers, was based on different kinds of categories which are laid out below:

Harm/care – Fairness/reciprocity – Ingroup/loyalty –
Authority/respect – Purity/sanctity
(Haidt, 2007; p 999 [extracted from Table 1])

For instance, Haidt cites 'disgust' as an example of the type of moral emotional response we might have to the violation of a well-established taboo which is covered by the 'Purity/sanctity' categories.

Other researchers have added evidence to the assumption that religious people tend to promote social welfare more than others. They reviewed several experiments to test the prosociality (charity) of religious believers as opposed to others and found that they were consistently more charitable. They explained this by suggesting that religious people had reputations to maintain, not only before their God but also within their faith communities. Their qualities of care and consideration for others survived because of the close-knit social networks of which they were part; whereas those who were dependent upon themselves for their values could more easily ignore the imperative to be 'good Samaritans'. Researchers have characterised faith communities in ways which may be summed up in the following quotation:

> In an intensely social, gossiping species, reputational concerns likely contributed to the evolutionary stability of strong cooperation between strangers. Individuals known to be selfish could be detected, subsequently excluded from future interaction, and even actively punished. (Norenzayan, *et al*; 2008; p 58)

Therefore, the individuals we are interested in as role models for a more compassionate and socially cohesive society may be those who hold values in common which come from their religious communities and upbringing. Unfortunately, what may have been lost in secular Britain are the ability and the desire of religious groups to put forward their point of view persuasively and authoritatively.

Actually, and as a final comment on these researches, to speak of 'conservatism' may be a misnomer because to choose rigorous palliative care in a familial home setting may be much more radical than an assisted suicide in which the family may be excluded by legal prohibitions.

We have become a much more atomised society in which the individual and his or her wishes are paramount. Life is judged by its quality – not communal qualities but individual aspirations and desires. We celebrate celebrity and think that the judgments we make about stars must also apply to ourselves. In death, we therefore celebrate life, exaggerating what qualities we have which in the slightest way measure up to the celebrities we read about. We are afraid of the ordinary and of the mundane achievements of bringing up families in a humdrum career which has no glamour but has borne the fruits of hard labour. Such lives are boring and without reward, or at least some think. Since most lives are now lived without the idea of salvation and redemption there can be little else to fret about. Public enemy number one is boredom and dissatisfaction which cannot be overcome by the transcendent worship of God. This is the stark picture of a society without faith and with a constant pressure to achieve one's own salvation.

The loss of love paints an equally gloomy picture. As families split up either because of divorce or the inevitable mobility of today's population we lose the very seedbed in which love is sown and nurtured. More and more people in society need help and care as the elderly grow older and disabled people have the opportunity to live fuller lives than was ever possible in the past. We know where the love is yet time after time it seems to be in short supply. We have lost what Reynolds calls 'the moral fabric of love'. (2008; p 123ff) In order to rediscover such a fabric we have to come close to those who are most in need, those who are vulnerable. Reynolds argues that we must come alongside disabled people and victims of all kinds of evils within our society and meet them in a spirit of love. Very often we simply take responsibility for such people as a duty – often a paid duty at that – and not in a spirit of love which may grow out of our family or religious fellowship. With the growth of the industry of care, responsibility becomes quantified and regulated until the guidance of love is eliminated. Medical staff are not allowed to pray with their patients and Christians may not show their faith in the outward symbol of a cross which may act as comfort to some passer-by. Responsibility deadens the joy of caring and places a cost on it. Such a cost can be exploited by both the carer and the caree in litigation which increases the need for bureaucracy.

The two strands come together in the intolerable pressure which some people feel at the end of their life when they feel that they are burdensome and that their families and society would be better without them.

How Modern Values Developed

Thus we come to the central part of the chapter. which is to examine more closely how religion has lost the battle to keep love and virtuous caring to the fore in the sure knowledge of salvation. Such an argument will be philosophical in nature and owes its origin to a book by Julian Young entitled *The Death of God and the Meaning of Life*. (2003) In it he shows how the meaning of life has changed over the centuries as the Platonic and then the Christian view of life has been supplanted by all those philosophies which developed towards and beyond the 'death of God'.

The modern philosophies Young examines are all from European writers of the 20th century who in different ways have rejected God as a guiding principle and have made men and women reliant upon themselves to live full and fulfilling lives. These, in turn, derived much from Schopenhauer and Nietzsche who died in 1900. We discover in the last chapter that Young's intention is to show how God can be rediscovered in a concern for the environment and a care for the way we treat it. Such a conclusion is not of great concern in the immediate context of life and death but his book does trace the history of certain popular ideas which circulate in the modern world and lead people to despair. Philosophy is often mirrored in popular culture and in the limits legislators are prepared to accept. This is particularly the case when individuals are vulnerable and weak with disease and a fear of the terrible future, which the media would have us believe is befalling more and more people in uncaring hospitals and overstretched nursing homes. Such thoughts and realities are beyond the scope of his book, so we will concentrate on identifying the characteristics of modern life which lead people to contemplate 'assisted suicide'.

There are great similarities between Platonic philosophies and Christianity, especially as formulated by Saint Paul. Both believe that we should envisage and aspire to what Young calls 'a real world'. In both writers, people were encouraged to aspire to something outwith themselves, something greater instead of being entirely dependent on internalised feelings of hopelessness and despair. Platonic love was more than just a non-sexual friendship, it was built on a deep respect and understanding of those whom we came in contact with.

> ... Platonic love, as we still say, referring to the fact that Plato's love is chaste, non-physical. Platonic love is a particular form of the philosophical life ...
> (Young, 2003; p 17)

The ideal society was held up to us as an image which was best described in Plato's metaphor of 'the cave'. From the darkness of the cave in which we are chained we can see the light of humanity living the perfect lives to which we should aspire. The goal of such a society was outwith us and something for which we had to strive. We strive because we recognise the good in a society governed by philosophers who would promote a just *polis* from which derives the word politics.

Christianity brought with it a similar aspiration to something greater than us. Salvation was offered through Christ who showed such a perfect life on this earth only to have it snatched from him on the cross, but redeemed for all of us in his resurrection and ascension to God's right hand.

St Paul brought systematic thought into the fledgling Christianity which was beginning to emerge in the days when he persecuted the movement. His thought brought great clarity to the beliefs of early Christians through the letters he wrote to communities of Christians. Three ideas seem to be important in this context: first, he distinguished between life under the law and living by grace; second, he believed, in this context, that we had to conquer our earthly desires; and third, he tried to persuade the communities he visited, particularly the Corinthians, that we had to live in organic unity.

Paul believed that we had lived our lives in accordance with the law which we could seldom fully obey and thus were guilty of sin. The law had been broken ever since the fall and yet '... as in Adam all die, so in Christ all will be made alive'. (1 Corinthians 15:22) By following Christ and accepting the gospel we are given the opportunity to live by grace free of the law and thus of death. Such grace carried with it all the best virtues of man's communal living and could only be achieved through belief in Jesus Christ.

Paul, however, accepted that this was difficult to achieve. Grace was neither a guaranteed state nor a guarantee of good behaviour but depended on our ability to subdue the passions of the flesh and of this world. Paul's perfect men and women were those who did precisely this through study and prayer. Yet, their failures were part of human nature – precisely that for which Jesus died to redeem. It was the same idea as Plato's perfect philosopher but was open to many and was always subject to the forgiveness of Christ. For many, in future generations Paul's disdain for the passions relegated his thought to the ramblings of a frustrated conservative. This was far from the case and Paul in fact offered a vision of a society which had an organic unity.

So finally, Paul presented the Corinthians with an image of 'the body' as a perfect example of society. The hands cannot do without the head or the head from the neck. Paul insisted that everyone has a role, in the same way different parts of our body have special functions and yet no part is superior to the next. They were linked by dependency and by the overall aim of society to revert to the metaphor. (1 Corinthians 12: 12–30)

Thus, Paul offers a very simple code by which Christians should live and which was accessible and freely available to a great many more people than Plato's elitism. We had to cast off the law in favour of a gospel of love and salvation. We were offered a code by which to live our own lives regarding our bodies as God's new temple and which was not to be defiled by baser instincts. Last and most importantly in the context of this book, we were called to recognise our interdependence on each other and the total futility of believing that we could do it all ourselves.

Such Christian beliefs were re-enforced by most of the Church Fathers from the early centuries right through to the Middle Ages. From Augustine to Aquinas the only deficit was that theology became more intellectualised and the preserve of the scholarly few. Whilst popular religion continued, philosophers pored over the remains of an over theologised God.

According to Young, Kant presented the last philosophical attempt to save Christianity from the European Enlightenment. I would exclude the Scottish Enlightenment from this mood of criticism of the tradition of Christianity which the Europeans believed was holding back progress in society. Kant insisted that Christianity was rational and that belief was a reality which had to be reckoned with.

> In a nutshell, Kant is claiming that Christian belief is 'rational' since, though we cannot prove it to be true, we need to validate the inescapable sense that there is a moral task to which we are committed – and hence a meaning to our lives.
> (Young, 2003; p 27)

When I read his *Critique of Practical Reason* in the late sixties, it brought me back from an obsession with the death of God and nihilism in general and set me on a journey which is not yet over. However, for most the death of God was more real and the works of Schopenhauer and Nietzsche ruled over modern thought.

Schopenhauer brought to the table the idea of boredom. Our lives had to transcend the boredom which can beset us. The thought of death may be attractive in a state of extreme boredom but it must be overcome. Schopenhauer had abolished any idea of God and could only answer suffering in a pseudo-Buddhist philosophy.

Nietzsche finally killed God off in two writings, one of which I quote:

> The madman jumped into their midst and pierced them with his eyes. "Whither is God?" he cried. "I shall tell you. *We have killed him*—you and I. All of us are his murderers. But how did we do this? How could we drink up the sea? Who gave us the sponge to wipe away the entire horizon? What were we doing when we unchained this earth from its sun? Whither is it moving now? Whither are we moving? Away from all suns? Are we not plunging continually? Backward, sideward, forward, in all directions? Is there any up or down left? Are we not straying as through an infinite nothing? Do we not feel the breath of empty space? Has it not become colder? Is not night continually closing in on us? ... God is dead. God remains dead. And we have killed him.... (*The Gay Science*, §125)

In a Godless world, the only salvation which remains available is our own heroic effort which may succeed or fail but puts tremendous strain upon ourselves and inflates or diminishes our egos as the case may be. It becomes a society which can be intolerably hard to live in, and our resources either often crack or we choose a way out of the suffering which Schopenhauer believed dominated society. Men and women now have an excuse to judge the quality of their own lives and to reach their own verdict, in a sure knowledge that there was no final judgement which was independent of their own ego. If we consider even later philosophers we find that death becomes an answer. An individual death can now be heroic and taken devoid of the feelings of others and outwith the control of a God who might shepherd us through the 'valley of the shadow of death'. (Psalm 23)

This compels us to consider one final philosopher, Heidegger who maintained that time was measured by death and that it was in our power to escape the drudgery of this life in our own death, by which we escape the unfortunate circumstances in which we find ourselves.

> Heidegger thinks that facing up to death is the key not only to autonomy, but also to focus. Facing and holding on to knowledge of our mortality (of death in the ontological richness of all of its three defining features) gives us autonomy *and focus at one and the same time.* {Italics original] (Young, 2003; p 117)

Time is given a meaning and a finality of measurement in death. Death can be the culmination of life in some heroic way or it can be the end of a fruitless existence of time frittered away or lost in a careless life. Death marks the end of our being in this world and offers a reality at the end of our lives. Heidegger's philosophy was very popular with some theologians and he was, for instance, a personal friend of Bultmann. (Young, 2003; p 113) We have discussed Ochs (above) who compellingly argues that our life as Christians should be a preparation for death and that we should live according to the precepts of Christ as we journey towards our ultimate end on this earth. He furthermore argues that death is always present it is not something we can put into the background as if it will never happen. Heidegger offered a vision of a heroic life in the values of ancient Rome and this was easily adapted by Christian theologians to a life spent in imitation of Christ. Even at its most innocuous, this philosophy tempted people to understand that death was something which they could control in certain circumstances of heroism.

Such a philosophy was to develop further in the work of Continental existentialists who recognised the deep dissatisfaction people may have with life and the opportunities death, or even suicide, could bring to someone who is suffering the deep despair of German *angst* or the *ennui* of the French writer, Satre. Satre wrote several books and novels in which he developed the idea of despair in lives complicated by distressing factors and complicated plots. Death in itself became an escape and a horrifying way in which life could be controlled. A very dangerous understanding of death was beginning to emerge. Boredom and suffering became an excuse for suicide, and it is not a big jump to consider that assisted suicide became a way out of the deep suffering of illness. These writers and books were masterful but dangerous and the plays which they have spawned both the material of masterpieces like *Waiting for Godot*; or countless popular dramas on TV that encouraged people to escape the trials of life in suicide.

The church has dealt with death throughout its existence and was well used to understanding the importance of preparing people for life after death. It has not, however, been as successful at counteracting the glamorization of suicide. Death is something we all wait for and in the process of waiting we can respond to the church's teaching, but in the case of suicide there is no waiting – it is our choice – and the church has failed to develop a convincing argument that it is wrong. Prescriptions no longer work. The church must seek an explanation which affirms the value of life and the ultimate condemnation of despair.

It is to this end that I believe Christians, and men and women of other faiths, must come up with an encouragement to life which overcomes the easy answer to despair. Such an answer, I believe lies in the values which Jesus treasured when he restored life. Of prime importance were family and kinship values which led to a mutual sustenance in times of economic adversity such as famine. In his miracles, his answer is not death but life, not egotism but community values. Finally, faith brought people through death, not to death, and it offers a celebration of life in whatever state beyond and before death. I think Jesus would have approved of *Christian Aid's* slogan, 'We believe in life before death', but he would not deny the equal importance of life after death.

The Public Face of Death

Before moving on to the next chapter dealing with assisted suicide, the question must be asked: how do people talk about life in death in the 21ˢᵗ century? My wife and I have an allotment which is about 100 yards away from one of Edinburgh's busiest crematoria. We are separated by only a high hedge. I believe that the allotments have been established on farmland which once belonged to the house which was adapted or demolished to accommodate the crematorium. If we spend a day at the allotment we often hear bagpipes playing a lament, often nothing at all, or lusty singing of hymns as opposed to the organ playing 'The Lord's my Shepherd' with no one joining in to sing. The enthusiastic Christian funeral is becoming rarer and even when we are separated by a hedge we can tell what kind of person is being buried. For instance, one day we listened to the funeral of an erstwhile *Boy's Brigade* officer. We knew because all the hymns were associated with that organisation and they were sung well by male voices. *Will your Anchor Hold in the Storms of Life?* We can often guess whether someone was of an evangelical persuasion or another kind of Christianity. I tell the story because it strikes me that some people can still proclaim their faith in death even if their relatives and minister are separated by a hedge and the limitations of our hearing. After such a day I often pray that there would be more people who would allow their faith to jump a hedge and speak even in death of their pilgrimage which is now at an end.

The growth of egotism has influenced the way we discuss our dying and place it in the context of salvation.

> In societies where identity is bound up largely with the group, what is feared is the demise of the group. But the more individualistic a culture, the more my own personal demise becomes problematic: 'In death, we fear we will lose our "I", our "me-ness". (Walter, 1994; p 16)

With the growth of a secular society many people have lost confidence in the concept of a soul. Our soul's onward journey into eternity is no longer the main concern of a funeral, and the liturgy which spoke of our onward journey has changed into a celebration of our lives. Funerals in the past were services of prayer and reflection on salvation but now they have become a celebration of a person's life. What one has achieved in life is reflected in death, and is often controlled by the deceased and produces copious instructions about how tributes are to be paid and by whom. The music reflects the taste of the deceased not the mourners. This works very well until we reflect that people are dying at older and older ages. An octogenarian may well not enjoy such a send off because those who might remember him or her have long since died themselves or are too incapacitated themselves to attend. (Davies, 2005; p 172) There is a notorious tendency for funerals at crematoria to become brief and impersonal and lost in the haste to keep up to the timetable for the day's list.

By contrast, celebrities and people who have enjoyed great public influence enjoy grand 'celebrations' of their lives or lavish memorial services which make lesser mortals quake as their achievements are lauded.

Just as many suffer the indignity of such hasty funerals, so many are remembered in private little ceremonies where a few relatives scatter ashes which will have no memorial other than the private memories of those who attend or choose the place. So much environmental damage is being done to the likes of Ben Nevis that a small park of remembrance has been established near the foot to discourage people from randomly covering the mountain, not only with ashes but personal mementos, in ways which were not envisaged. Such private memories are yet another sign of a willingness to entrust everything to our own will and power rather than to God.

Kate Berridge warns against such personal control of funeral rites because they result in our desire to hold on to our self rather than release our life to others and to God.

> We have lost the art of transcendence. How to forget yourself is the concept we need to reclaim. (Berridge, 2001; p 242)

And as cemeteries and books of remembrances become diminished, so our confidence to witness to a collective religious belief system and awareness of our common humanity disappears. As Walter puts it:

> By the late twentieth century it is becoming fashionable in some circles to scatter cremation ashes in a special place known only to close family. Communal resurrection has thus given way via the family tomb to private memories—a process not only of secularisation, but also of ever growing individualism and privacy. (Walter, 1994; p 15)

This inability to let go of our self in death extends to life. We are no longer able to comprehend the mystery of sustaining love which can be found in family life and in marriage and offers the very real chance for us to live, even in the face of severe suffering as a result of illness. This is where it becomes important for the Church to try to enable people to live in bonds of love which transcend the immediate longing for death, which is a natural thought for us all but can become an obsession in some.

Chapter VII

To Cherish or Abandon Life

> Switzerland, Ziegler claims, has consumed more peace and democracy than it has produced. Neutrality has provided a convenient smokescreen - although it should be pointed out that there are few nations on earth which have not benefited from this neutrality. Even those suicide tourists who end up on trestles in Swiss morgues can avail themselves of its privileges. You can arrive at the Zurich apartment of Dignitas in the afternoon, and be dead by the evening. The organisation is the epitome of neutralism, providing as it does an exit from this world unhindered by awkward examinations of conscience. (Saunders, 2003; p 33)

This chapter is about my contention that 'assisted suicide' offends God's implied core values of life as illustrated in the miracles that have been discussed. These actual values will be briefly reiterated in the final chapter. I am not an expert on euthanasia or palliative care and cannot offer a wide ranging review of the ethical issues involved. It seems sensible, therefore, to consider only one issue and to draw conclusions from it. In the last decade, many people from the UK have travelled to Switzerland to be assisted to die by a charity, albeit an expensive charity, in a flat near Zurich. Zurich is one of the most liberal cantons in Switzerland. *Dignitas* has offered to some a way out of what they consider to be intolerable lives by filling a gap which they find lacking in the UK. It is impossible in this country to ask a physician to prepare a lethal dose of drugs which will result in rapid but painless death. People have thus been forced to make doleful 'tourist' trips to Zurich and some have recorded their final experience to be shared on network television.

Having admitted that I am not qualified to discuss this subject in great depth, do I have any personal qualifications? I have cerebral palsy which is not in itself either a degenerative or painful condition but is one which shows up more difficulties with age. As I age, now 63 years, my mobility and dexterity have deteriorated but not to any extent that makes me want to end my life now or in the foreseeable future. I am sustained by the love of a wonderful wife and many supportive family members.

However, I do understand the cries of those who want to legalise assisted suicide. I have gone through episodes when the attraction of death has been great. As a pubescent teenager I cried myself to sleep on many occasions as my raging hormones longed for a girlfriend I was never going to get because of my disability. When I was fourteen a schoolmate, Colin, died of pneumonia after a fairly standard operation to release his legs which were becoming more and more tense and making it impossible to go to the toilet or anything else. Colin had no speech and could not do anything for himself but nevertheless was extremely intelligent and could show off his ability to do mental arithmetic which was certainly beyond me. As a callous teenager I said to my mother that I wished it had been me that had died not him. My mother went into a sullen kind of shocked silence for several days. Throughout my life I have set such suicidal thoughts aside when I considered the sustaining love of my family – where it had brought me and where it might still lead me; and gratitude for that love which I had received and might still offer.

I remember also attending a meeting of *Exit* at a conference of free thinkers near London in my early thirties. I was very excited at the prospect of attending this meeting and having all my support for euthanasia confirmed and informed by experts. The truth is that I cannot remember attending such an unloving meeting in my life. It was absolutely devoid of feeling for others and love for those near to you. I have much the same feelings now when I read articles by Dr Ludwig A. Minelli of *Dignitas* whilst recognizing that he is endeavouring to be compassionate and caring.

I also opposed a motion in the General Assembly of the *Church of Scotland* which anathematized euthanasia and lost. I would have to say that I think that dogmatic opposition to anything is wrong because I will never say, never. Even so, I now oppose the legalization proposing the blanket decriminalisation of assisted suicide.

Like, I imagine many disabled people, I have dark moods when I feel that I would be better off dead than alive or I dread a prolonged and undignified death. I found it difficult living on an Orkney island for ten years surrounded by a tempestuous sea which betokened a watery and cold end. It is when these moods become obsessions that the enormous energy which is required to campaign and fight for new legislation comes to the fore.

Margaret Somerville has written an interesting book entitled *Death Talk: The Case Against Euthanasia and Physician-Assisted Suicide* in which she discusses the nature of the way we discuss euthanasia. She confirms my own belief that the language we use is ambiguous. 'Euthanasia' literally means 'a good death'. This is something we all aspire to, and probably we would further aspire to slipping away in our sleep with no pain and no disruption to our dignity. Every death is a bad death in that it is sad, but the term can only be used very broadly to signify our abhorrence of violent deaths and deaths which in some way highlight the loneliness some people live in. The problem with a good death is that the term is used by both those in favour of euthanasia and those against.

> It is interesting that people who advocate the legalization of euthanasia, as well as some of those who oppose doing so, have argued for a wide definition. They propose that it should include all medical interventions or non-interventions that would shorten life or that would not prolong it. But each group has adopted this position for exactly the opposite reason. The pro-choice group argue for a broad definition in order to allow all interventions or non-interventions that would promote a "good death," including those undertaken with the primary intention of killing people. Some of those who oppose euthanasia (especially some pro-life groups) argue for a broad definition in order to prohibit all interventions or non-interventions that would shorten life – not

only those undertaken with the primary intention of killing people. (Somerville, 2002; p 25)

Pro-life groups stress the benefits of palliative care as a successful way of reducing pain and offering dignity in the last days of a person's life. Although it is changing slowly, palliative care has mainly been offered to those suffering from terminal cancer. Hopefully the day will come when such care will be offered to people with degenerative illnesses such as motor neurone disease. To be opposed to euthanasia does not prevent the withdrawal of futile treatment or offering pain relief which will ultimately hasten death. Such actions are not aimed at producing death which is the difference between them and physician assisted suicide. Likewise, pro-life groups have no need to oppose a decision to decline resuscitation if it is well thought out before the event becomes an inevitability. To aim for a good death is to aim for the relief of pain, offering dignity in illness and the opportunity to be with loved ones either at home or in a hospice.

Those who favour euthanasia believe that death should be controlled by the individual at a time of their own choosing and preferably before all that is left is palliative care. Their language is very similar. There is a charity in Britain called *Friends at the End* (FATE). Such a name illustrates the great similarity in language and competition to prove compassion. FATE offers advice and help on suicide but at the same time suggests that you are surrounded by like-minded friends who will be with you at the last – in thought at least. The 'good death' is one which is controlled and where the patient parting from loved ones becomes the gathering of a couple of relatives in Switzerland who will share your last moments in a death process which may last a couple of hours, although with little more than five minutes' consciousness on the part of 'the patient'.

Somerville argues that the popular support for euthanasia suggests a new way of talking about death. Death may now be controlled by the individual. It is an avoidance of the end which may be indeterminate in length and style. She also points out that such control is an illusion. In countries where there is legalised euthanasia, people may feel threatened by doctors who have been offered yet another level of control when dealing with vulnerable people either in their last days or if severely disabled, as in Holland. (Somerville, 2002; p 31) If such a desire to control death exists, it exhibits a tremendous lack of faith in the love which could sustain them in a society geared towards palliative care.

Ironically, control also was and remains the key to palliative care and the pioneering work of Cicely Saunders in the early developments in the hospice movement in London. Her aim, firstly as a nurse and then as a doctor, was to seek to control pain by new, and higher, dosages of pain killers than had been previously used in what was thought to be safe doses. (Have & Clark, 2002; p 20) She also planned to give patients and family members sufficient control over their environment either in hospital or at home to control the last days of the patient's time with their loved ones. The palliative care literature has always been family oriented but in recent years it has been increasingly difficult to define the family and 'significant others' who may have a role in the closing days of someone's life. There has to be a flexible approach to people's wishes for how they wish to spend the remainder of their life and sufficiently skilled counsellors and chaplains on hand to help people work through their fears, regrets and unfinished business at the end of their life. Saunders was a religious person and the early hospice movement had strong Christian influences. This has unfortunately become diluted with the onward march of secularism. The main point was that there was a strong motive to control symptoms sufficiently to allow patients to benefit from such spiritual input and family love. The sustenance of love was sufficient to bring relief of symptoms without medical intervention.

I would, however, criticise the hospice movement for building up such a strong emphasis on cancer. Only recently, have other terminal conditions been given much attention. This has perhaps lead many people down the assisted suicide route, perhaps feeling that they will derive no benefit from a hospice or the charities such as *Macmillan* and *Marie Curie* which have a reputation for dealing with cancer. To where do disabled people turn?

The laws governing assisted suicide are complex and beyond my discussion. There are places such as Oregon in America and Holland where physician assisted suicide have been legalised but elsewhere the situation is often unsatisfactory or ambiguous. I shall look at simply England, Scotland and Switzerland to understand some of these complications.

In England it is a crime to assist or abet suicide. To do so, incurs a fourteen year prison sentence. Such prosecutions are rare because there is a reluctance to prosecute exercised mercy in the interests of a loved one. The Scottish law is very ambiguous. Assisting a suicide is illegal but there is no fixed penalty. A mercy killing is most likely to result in a prosecution for culpable homicide (manslaughter) which may result in a harsh sentence, even perhaps be elevated to murder; or a light suspended sentence. When I attended the meeting of *Exit* in London they were excited at the prospect of publishing their handbook in Scotland whereas it would have been illegal in England. Irrespective of my views on euthanasia, I applaud Scotland's much more compassionate approach to crime and punishment. It is not a legitimate criticism of Scotland's system to suggest that the quality of mercy is randomly dispensed by the judiciary. Such a variety of judgements must act both as a source of compassion and deterrent. This principle seems to be becoming practice in the *Director of Public Prosecution's* (DPP) attitude to the application of English law.

In some respects, Switzerland's law on euthanasia is not as liberal as we perhaps think. It has been made liberal by the fact that physicians are allowed on their conscience to write a prescription for a lethal dose of barbiturates but are not allowed to administer it. Direct administration of a lethal injection by a doctor is illegal. Also, the law so far has not prohibited people from travelling from the UK or elsewhere. Switzerland is the only country with permissive legislation which allows non-residents to avail themselves of such services. The laws were intended to help those with terminal illnesses but they have been used by people with chronic disabilities. This ability to travel, to become 'euthanasia tourists', is perhaps an unintended consequence of their laws. The law is quite explicitly opposed to exploitation of the vulnerable and weak.

> ... Whoever, from selfish motives, induces another person to commit suicide or aids him in it, shall be confined in the penitentiary for not over five years, or in the prison, provided that the suicide has either been completed or attempted. (Article 115 of the Swiss Criminal Code)

Each country which has been mentioned seeks to protect the vulnerable, people with mental health problems or with learning difficulties, and Switzerland has thus far insisted that some written intentions on the part of the person seeking to die must exist, especially if they have lost capability in the recent past. *Dignitas* encourages members to sign up when they feel inclined towards the end which they offer. There is a handsome membership fee and higher charges when death is actually achieved. Members can be looking at a bill of around £4000, which never seems to come into the public discussion. The charity seeks to ascertain that the person who is seeking help is of sound mind and can accept membership quite a long time in advance of any action. It is thus best suited to people who have a dogmatic view of what may be their intended end.

The Swiss Federal Legislature has recently sought to clamp down on 'suicide tourists' travelling to Switzerland. Forthcoming legislation will insist that two physicians will have to certify that the patient is terminally ill and is of sound enough mind to seek to die. Chronic illnesses will be discounted. "'It won't be possible in future for someone to cross the border and commit suicide a few days later with the help of an organisation," Ms Widmer-Schlumpf [the Swiss Justice Minister] said.' (*The Times*, October 29, 2009) Interestingly, it is proposed to legislate that more money be spent on palliative care which has been neglected in the country.

At present, the doctor who prescribes the lethal dose does not have to see the patient. In future he will be expected to interview the patient twice before prescribing the medication. This will mean that, along with the independent assessments, the patient will be required to spend some time in Switzerland prior to actually receiving assistance to commit suicide. This ought to deter many.

The move against 'treating' people with chronic illnesses is also very welcome. A major step towards allowing anyone to die was taken when a young rugby player went to *Dignitas* with his family. Daniel James who had a playing career ahead of him was paralysed from the neck down when a rugby scrum collapsed on top of him. He was treated at Stoke Mandeville Hospital for spinal injuries. A spokesman said that he was surprised at the speed with which Daniel had come to a decision. It normally takes a long time for tetraplegics to come to terms with the new state of their life but usually counselling and intensive therapy brings them through this stage. The problem with Daniel James' case was that he was not chronically ill and had many years of life, with improvements expected, ahead of him.

The banning of chronic illnesses will severely restrict many who might wish to use the services of *Dignitas*. Debbie Purdy suffers from multiple sclerosis and at present enjoys a full life with her husband but she is fearful of future deterioration which would further restrict her independence to travel to Switzerland unassisted. In a case brought firstly before the High Court in proceedings which started in June, 2008, she argued that the law should be made clear as to whether her husband would be prosecuted for assisting her at some future date in travelling to Zurich. She was aware that many people have been questioned after the suicide of a loved one in Switzerland but very few have been prosecuted. This again is an example of the uncertainty principle which leaves doubts in people's minds as to whether their assistance will result in a prosecution. The parents of Daniel James were interviewed by the police at length before a decision was made not to prosecute.

New Guidelines Governing Prosecution in England and Wales

Most of these decisions are made on the grounds of public interest and the *Crown Prosecution Service* has had over the years very little appetite to prosecute people who acted from what they considered to be the best motives for their loved one. Juries are similarly reluctant to return guilty verdicts. Purdy took her case to a final appeal at the House of Lords demanding that the law be clarified, that the lottery of whether or not one was prosecuted be ended and some clarification of the legal guidelines offered by the *Director of Public Prosecutions*, Keir Starmer QC, for England and Wales be given and enforced. In 2009 the Law Lords instructed the DDP to clarify the *Crown Prosecution Service's* policy in an expeditious but appropriate way. He chose to publish an interim statement September 2009 outlining a provisional policy followed by a final complete statement within a reasonable time following public consultation based on it. (CPS, 2009)

In upholding the appeal by Debbie Purdy against the decision of the High Court in the House of Lords, Lord Hope of Craighead wrote:

> The cases that have been referred to the Director are few, but they will undoubtedly grow in number. Decisions in this area of the law are, of course, highly sensitive to the facts of each case. They are

also likely to be controversial. But I would not regard these as reasons for excusing the Director from the obligation to clarify what his position is as to the factors that he regards as relevant for and against prosecution in this very special and carefully defined class of case. How he goes about this task must be a matter for him, as also must be the ultimate decision as to whether or not to prosecute. But, as the definition which I have given may show, it ought to be possible to confine the class that requires special treatment to a very narrow band of cases with the result that the Code will continue to apply to all those cases that fall outside it.

I would therefore allow the appeal and require the Director to promulgate an offence-specific policy identifying the facts and circumstances which he will take into account in deciding, in a case such as that which Ms Purdy's case exemplifies, whether or not to consent to a prosecution under section 2(1) of the 1961 Act.

(Opinions of The Lords of Appeal for Judgment in the Cause: R (on the application of Purdy) (Appellant) v Director of Public Prosecutions (Respondent))

The DDP's *Interim Report* states at the outset that he is not responsible for changing the law which states that to assist a suicide remains a crime. The next Law Lord to give an opinion, Baroness Hale of Richmond, referred to a speech in a House of Lords debate by Lord McKay of Clashfern, a man well-known for his profound Christian faith and convictions, on 7th July 2009. Having read it, he seems to support the principle of uncertainty which has been alluded to twice before. He said, '... a change in the law that would deprive vulnerable people, at a vulnerable stage in their lives, of a protection that the law currently affords. *The fear of prosecution is quite an important aspect of the prevention of crime in many of our arrangements.* (Lords Hansard, 7 Jul 2009; Volume 712, Column 600)

We will examine some of the *Interim Statement* shortly but it is important to note that the DPP made it quite clear that it was not for him but for Parliament to alter the law and whatever guidance he offered could not alter the fact that assisting a suicide was a crime. The House of Lords has witnessed an abortive attempt to alter the law, and it remains to be seen whether Margo Macdonald MSP's Bill in Scotland will receive sufficient support from a Scottish Parliament which has a considerable number of MSPs with a religious background or who are dependent upon Roman Catholic votes in the west of Scotland. Thus, the law remains unaltered in England but may have been clarified in a way which will probably beckon more legislation at Westminster. However, it would probably be dependent on a backbencher's Private Bill in the House of Commons with Government time and a free vote. Some have argued that the law has been changed in so far as the DPP has been forced to codify the criteria which will influence whether a prosecution takes place or not. Keir Starmer argues that the law already required that every case be referred to his office prior to a prosecution, and that all the Law Lords had required was that the criteria be laid down in a code of practice rather than remain dependent on the random actions of the DPP. This however removes the element of uncertainty which acts as a deterrent and reflects our current society's desire to see everything written in black and white with little room for deviation.

Of greater concern is the creeping influence of 'consulted' public opinion which seems to be supplanting the importance of both legislators and the judiciary. Margo Macdonald, who is an independent member of the *Scottish Parliament* and has Parkinson's Disease, has tried to mobilise public opinion in favour of physician assisted suicide through 'consultations', and the DPP may unwittingly have done the same. The DPP has always had to protect the 'public interest'. He asserts that 'Prosecutors must consider the public interest factors set out in the Code for Crown Prosecutors and the factors set out in this policy.' However, should the 'public interest' in potential criminal cases be decided by consultation? If it must then Christian opinion must be heard. The Christian community fails to realise that much modern legislation, such as rights for homosexuals, has been promulgated with the help of what

I call 'pre-emptive consultation'. By such processes, non-secular views tend to be marginalised.

The consultation document produced by the DPP takes a compassionate but strict view of the nature of permissible, or understandable, assisted suicide. What the document says is not dissimilar to the views expressed by *Dignitas* and by many others who support assisted suicide. This is a product of the confusion shown by the desire of all to be seen to be compassionate in distressing circumstances. The DPP recommends that a prosecution might occur if it was shown that the accused had solicited a person's will to commit suicide or has done so because of some gain to be made by the person's death. No one under the age of 18 would be considered suitable for an assisted suicide, neither would anyone suffering from mental incapacity or illness. Thus far both sides would seem to agree. Starmer sets forth thirteen scenarios where he would not prosecute and sixteen where he would.

The real source of disagreement lies in the acceptance of the DPP of the fact that a person may have a settled will to die, and if this is because of a terminal illness for which there is no cure that person has certain rights to have access to a humane death. As one who opposes such deaths, I would argue that such individuals must be encouraged to understand that there are qualities to human life which may sustain you through such trials and reward you with the experience of true love at the end of one's life. What the new guide-lines do is tip the balance towards the opposite argument, that they have a right to a dignified death at a time and place of their choosing.

The DPP received over 4,000 representations to the consultation. A sizeable number of those will have come from churches and people of Christian conviction. Such choices are often made without moral consideration of values which Christians may hold and may well be a reaction to church dogma which can feel very stern and devoid of compassion.

The final report of the *Crown Prosecution Service* was published on 25th January, 2010. It has responded to the public consultation but it is hard to see much that is different from the *Interim Statement* of 2009. It remains a criminal offence to aid and abet someone's suicide and there is no suggestion that such an offence should be decriminalised. The vulnerable are protected in so far as they are either young, mentally incapacitated or may be a source of gain to someone who may benefit from their death. The document makes it very clear that no professional, be that a doctor or a carer, may be involved in assisting such a suicide. This is very welcome and makes it clear that vulnerable people will be protected whilst under the care of either the medical services or social services. Prosecutions will not proceed where there is no evidence to suggest that any of the above have been breached in any material way. The guidelines make 'compassion' their guiding principle. Has someone assisted a suicide in the knowledge that that person had a clear and settled will to die and had expressed this on many occasions? The problem is that compassion is not a legal term. It is one of these ambiguous words which can be used by those who favour assisted suicide and those who are against. Compassion is a central ethic of Christianity and also of other religions. Christians would argue that palliative care is compassionate and that the skills which can bring dignity in the final days of a person's life are much more profound than the compassion of someone who assists a suicide.

This report and policy challenges the churches to advocate and commend their understanding of compassion as a higher calling than the compassion which may allow someone to avoid prosecution. The law as it stands will be upheld but the opportunities for 'do-gooding' have never been greater. The churches must assert the values which have been discussed here and divert people from the easy compassion which may lead to suicide. The debate will all be about motives and this surely is the central work of the church.

It is interesting that Margo Macdonald's Bill before the *Scottish Parliament* does involve both medical practitioners and experts in determining the eligibility of someone seeking to die. It also permits physicians to facilitate euthanasia if it is sanctioned by the panel. It would appear that this is a move too far even to contemplate in the English legislation, and is likely to be so when the final vote is taken in the Scottish Parliament which may be very soon.

In each case under any of the jurisdictions that have been discussed, someone has to ask for the assistance of someone else, probably a loved one. It is an awesome responsibility to take a life even with a compassionate motive, and to live with it long after your loved one has been released from all the burdens of this life. Jesus restored life to endless opportunities; he never ended it.

The last chapter will draw together God's value of life in a way that avoids dogmatism and unequivocal arguments which so often alienate non-Christians. The issue is a matter which ought to unite all the Abrahamic religions, if the arguments can be forwarded with compassion and concern for people who are undoubtedly suffering greatly in their dying days, or as they see their condition deteriorate from a tolerable disability to an intolerable illness.

Conclusion

Re-stating God's Values

God is a God of compassion who is slow to show anger and has abundantly shown his capacity to love in the gift of his son Jesus Christ. We act in his best interests when we take guidance from his rules of compassion and love. Yet the Churches very often dwell on his negative and angrier rules and guidance. In this chapter his compassion will be shown in the way we can infer his values from the miracles of resuscitation and how they may be applied to the question of assisted suicide. However, the easiest sources of guidance display God's more angry side and the Churches' love for dogmatic rules.

There are two such dogmas which must be dealt with first. The first is, you shall not kill; and the second concerns the value of suffering as one path to salvation.

The sixth commandment forbids us to kill but we have already seen that the word 'kill' can lead to many controversies. We are really forbidden to murder and this imposes on us a debate about what is murder. A majority of Americans believe that it is wrong to kill a foetus but are equally willing to support capital punishment, which is not only a death sentence but quite often involves suffering during the execution. If it is correct that we are forbidden to murder this means that we are forbidden to take a life illegally or in a way which is incompatible with the love of God. Laura Schlessinger, a right wing American, argues that murder is an offence to God every time it is committed, and she goes on to attack legalised abortion and at the same time defends capital punishment. She considers that suicide is an offence before God and of course applies this to assisted suicide, otherwise euthanasia. In her opinion, both the person wishing to die and anyone contemplating assisting are offending God and his creation.

RE-STATING GOD'S VALUES

> On the issue of euthanasia, Judaism, Catholicism, and some other Christian denominations are in agreement that active euthanasia is forbidden because it is murder. Active euthanasia, however noble the motive, can never be condoned, even if intended solely for the purpose of ending the suffering of a patient. Even if the individual asks for assistance in terminating his or her life, it is forbidden because of the issues we have discussed earlier in the chapter, including that we are made in the image of God and suicide is expressly prohibited.
> (Schlessinger, 1989; p 193)

She reserves most of her attack for the State of Oregon. More general thinking has spawned such theories as the just war and has now extended to a whole variety of circumstances where human life is taken in a way which is legal. The argument, therefore, must be that if the government legislates to make assisted suicide legal it is no longer a breach of the commandment. I believe that such an argument has compelling logic and that we must therefore look for other illustrations of God's love of life to persuade those who might favour assisted suicide to think again.

The second argument is equally fraught with difficulties. Jesus said that we must take up his cross and follow him, and many people have interpreted this as suggesting that we must suffer personally as he did upon the cross and throughout his passion. Such an argument is very old, and unlike the last argument has the support of many who need to make sense of their own suffering and accept it for the sake of Jesus. To argue against this is to potentially hurt people who need the support of such a doctrine to help them through their suffering. Nevertheless, it is an argument that is flawed and must be put to rest gently and over time.

Jesus prepared his disciples for their future suffering as he travelled to Jerusalem to face his own passion. His ministry has been noted by its concern to relieve personal suffering, and his miracles were a testimony to his belief that illness and disease should be relieved by every compassionate means possible. Jesus travelled to Jerusalem with another agenda of showing that through his suffering on the cross a good or salvation would become available to those who believed in him. His suffering was one of choice, a choice from which he tried to escape when he begged his father to release him in the Garden of Gethsemane. He also warned disciples like Peter that they would suffer the agonies of crucifixion if they obeyed his commands – by implication, the great commission to go forth and baptise. The suffering Jesus had in mind was not the personal suffering which comes to us when we are ill or down on our fortunes but the suffering we take upon ourselves when we espouse the cause of Jesus and act for the sake of the gospel. I, therefore, wish to abandon the argument that it is meritorious to suffer in illness as if the affliction in some way reflected the will of Jesus.

Therefore, let us turn to the values which Jesus displayed in his miracles. These values call us to imitate him as humanity, not as individuals with our own agendas and concerns. First, let us list the values which have come out in the previous chapters:

1. Suffering can be most readily eased if it is within in the institution of the family or close relationships.
2. Love is capable of sustaining us when we are pushed to the extreme.
3. Jesus has a great concern for our economic welfare which can suffer in bereavement.
4. No matter how long the ordeal lasts, God will remain to provide sustenance in the face of adversity.

In each of the miracle pericopes which were considered the suffering of bereavement, be it that of emotional loss or other forms of deprivation, took place in the context of close relationships. Most involved family but Eutychus died in the context of religious fellowship, and Tabitha both in the fellowship of Christ and in close relationship with other women involved in mission. We noted how much Jesus was emotionally involved in Lazarus' family. In each case the anticipation of mourning was made more bearable by the solidarity of a small group of people gathered around either to witness the death or comfort the central mourners. God leaves it perfectly clear to us that our emotions must be shared with others and our deepest concerns expressed to them. Love is the ideal setting and emotion for dealing with the trauma of death and illness.

Yet love is such a complex emotion that we complicate the way we harness it when we are confronted by the suffering and death of a loved one. The flaws of loving relationships can surface at such times. A loving partner may wish to offer altruistic care to a dying loved one who may push away such care, thinking that he or she is a burden. (Gunderson, 2004) Generally people who covenant to love one another do so in the expectation that they will think similarly, but often this is not the case. To reject care may be exceedingly hurtful and one might suggest that those who wish to die are opting out of the relationship. The church has to reinforce the value of love and prepare people for the hard times of life as well as teaching them how to share the good times. By and large, the desire to seek euthanasia is to assert one's ego over everyone else's. There are families who have accompanied loved ones to die in Zurich in complete harmony but it is surely the case that their actions are driven by the determination of the dying person. The law, mercifully, appears to penalise only those who lead a person to death for selfish or economic reasons.

In countries such as America, health care is so expensive that this adds another dimension to the temptation to see one's life as a burden or be treated as a burden.

It is natural to assume that greater and greater dependency does impose a burden on others but in many cases such a perception appears to be wrong. McGrath and Newell (2004) studied the emotions of carers towards the end of a person's life, and found that a great sense of satisfaction came to the carer and a complete identification with the deteriorating condition of the dying one. Their account of the carer's feelings gives great hope that people can and will offer altruistic care. In the relationship between Georgina and her carer there was a great deal of spirituality that held them together, and a sense of humour and mutual respect gave the dignity to life which so many fear losing. The case-study shows clearly that despite society's wish to deny the reality of death and disability there can be great strength in the mature bonding in this very intimate relationship which is leading to the death of one. The palliative care movement has traditionally been based on the involvement of the family, where hospice staff can help to teach people the new relationships which become necessary in these last months and days. If the Church has a real intention to proclaim family values it must be at the centre of people's struggles with the conflict between their own autonomy which encourages them to think either only of themselves and relationships which they feel they will be unable to develop with willing loved ones at such a time. Gunderson describes beautifully the delicate dance of reciprocity, or lack of it, in a relationship:

> It is difficult to see how a relationship can flourish when each partner refuses caring help from the other, even when in fact, particularly when it concerns centrally important needs such as health care. Each may still be prepared to help the other, but the reciprocity is lost. Each is saying, in effect, I will care for you, but will not accept help from you. (Gunderson, 2004; p 39)

God has time after time illustrated that love can prevail and that it can develop in very difficult circumstances. Loving relationships can ease the pain of departing and lighten the drudgery of caring. Nevertheless, reciprocity must exist and flourish even in the most difficult of circumstances.

If we look at the miracles of Elisha and Elijah, it becomes obvious that God's care stretches far beyond the miracle of bringing the sons back to life. The bereaved women require to be looked after in poverty, in hardship and in legal disputes. He is always there. We must preach that God's comfort and care will be present in the final stages of life if we remain in the love which he has given us and the strength which his peace can offer. The problem is that so few people wish to hear such a message today and would rather rely on their own autonomy to see them through to an assisted suicide. The suffering is not going to be that of pain or indignity but the refusal to believe that the blessings of love will be sustained throughout this difficult period.

Last, if we expect people to have the right to die in loving relationships we must ensure that we act as God's hands in providing the wherewithal to meet the costs involved in palliative care. This is now the ongoing debate in Switzerland and it will always be a debate in this country, until we realise that everyone has a right to dignity at the end and not the indignity of a hospital ward which is understaffed and often death denying until the very last minute.

Epilogue

> But he [the Lord] said to me, "My grace is sufficient for you, for my power is made perfect in weakness." Therefore I will boast all the more gladly about my weaknesses, so that Christ's power may rest on me. (2 Corinthians 12:9)

I believe that the key to the whole debate that surrounds the miracles where people have been brought back to life. and the debate about euthanasia have a common key which does not emanate directly from them.

As human beings we are not very good at accepting gifts and usually like to reciprocate by returning a similar gift. The entire story of God's dealing with mankind can be seen as his showering of gifts upon us which we cannot reciprocate and cannot match in any way. Similarly, human kindness often offers gifts which cannot be returned.

God first of all gave us the gift of life in the act of creation. To live and work with such a gift requires grace, and the gospel is full of the consciousness of the gift God gave in his only son. Jesus graciously accepted the burden of persecution and death to fulfil the gift of salvation to all who receive him. The harmony of Jesus with God, his father, is proclaimed by John boldly in terms of grace, 'The Word became flesh and made his dwelling among us. We have seen his glory, the glory of the One and Only, who came from the Father, full of grace and truth'. (John 1:14) We can only respond by accepting with similar grace the gift of life and understand that human love is a reflection of this gift.

When Paul wrote the words that are quoted at the beginning he was downhearted because of the 'thorn in his flesh' – an illness which troubled and even depressed him. He responded, however, to the free gift of faith in the one who had purchased his salvation on the cross and in the fellowship of faith communities in which he ministered.

When God restored life to those in the miracles he did not ask for reward, but one must assume that some of them had the grace to accept the gift of life which had been given to all of us but had been offered in a special way to them. To live as a created individual child of God must be done so in a spirit of grace and acceptance of the gift which can never be repaid.

I had a lecturer at the University of Edinburgh in New College, J B Torrance, who unjustifiably earned the catch phrase, 'take my wife' whom he used in lectures by way of illustration. He would then go on to explain to us how she cooked and looked after the house for him and never counted the cost. His acceptance of her gift was like the acceptance of grace. If it is correct to maintain that love will sustain a person through a terminal illness and difficult suffering, it is necessary to reiterate the value of grace and the fact that it is freely given. To receive it is difficult but rewarding. We forget today that our autonomy should not supersede all the love which may surround us at a time of suffering. If the church can make a contribution to rebalancing people's attitude, there might be less desire for the individual to take absolute and final control in euthanasia.

Bibliography

Barth, K., 2005, *God Here and Now*, Routledge Classics, London

Berridge, K., 2001, *Vigor Mortis: The End of the Death Taboo*, Profile Books, London

Bolt, P. G., 2003, *Jesus' Defeat of Death: Persuading Mark's Early Readers*, Cambridge University Press, Cambridge

Bovon, F., 2006, *Luke the Theologian: Fifty-five Years of Research (1950–2005)*, Baylor University Press, Waco, Tex.

Clarke, G. W., 1974, *The Octavius of Marcus Minucius Felix*, Newman Press, New York

Corner, M., 2005, *Signs of God: Miracles and Their Interpretation*, Ashgate Publishing, Aldershot

Cupitt, D., 2003, *Life, Life*, Polebridge Press, Santa Rosa, CA

Davies, D. J., 2005, *A Brief History of Death*, Blackwell, London

DPP, 2009, *Interim Policy for Prosecutors in respect of Cases of Assisted Suicide*, Crown Prosecution Service, London

Eichrodt, W., 1970, *Ezekiel: A Commentary*, Westminster Press, Philadelphia

Evans (trans.), E., 1960, *Tertullian's Treatise on the resurrection*, Uncatalogued, London

Grabbe, L. L., 1997, *Human and the Divine in History*, Continuum International Publishing, London

Gray, J., 1963, *I & II Kings: A Commentary*, Westminster Press, Philadelphia

Gunderson, M., 2004, 'Being a Burden: Reflections on Refusing Medical Care', *The Hastings Center Report*, Vol 34, No 5

Guthrie, S., 2005, 'Back to Life', *The Christian Century*, Vol 122, No 5, March 8

Haidt, *et al*, J., 2007, 'The New Synthesis in Moral Psychology', *Science*, Vol 316, 998

Have & Clark, H. T. & D., 2002, *The Ethics of Palliative Care: European Perspectives*, Open University Press, Philadelphia

Hick, J., 1966, *Evil and the God of Love*, Macmillan, London

Howarth, G., 2007, *Death & Dying*, Polity, Cambridge

BIBLIOGRAPHY

Hunsinger, G., 2000, 'Karl Barth's Christology: Its basic Chalcedonian character', *Webster, op cit,*

Hunter, A. M., 1968, *According to John*, SCM Press, London

Hurtado, L. W., 2005, *Lord Jesus Christ: Devotion to Jesus in Earliest Christianity*, Wm. B. Eerdmans Publishing, Grand Rapids

Kellehear, A., 2007, *A Social History of Dying*, Cambridge University Press, Cambridge

Keown, J., 2002, *Euthanasia, Ethics and Public Policy: An Argument Against Legalisation*, Cambridge University Press, Cambridge

Kinlaw, P. E., 2005, *Christ is Jesus: Metamorphosis, Possession, and Johannine Christology*, Society of Biblical Literature, Atlanta, GA

Kleinman, A., 1998, *The Illness Narratives*, Basic Books, New York

Krantz, S. L., 2002, *Refuting Peter Singer's Ethical Theory*, Praeger, Westport, CT

Levenson, J. D., 2006, *Resurrection and the Restoration of Israel*, Yale University Press, New Haven

Lewis, C. S., 1961/1996, *A grief observed*, HarperCollins Publishers, New York

Lightfoot, R. H., 1956, *St. John's Gospel: A Commentary*, Clarendon Press, Oxford

Markham, I. S., 1999, *Plurality and Christian Ethics*, Seven Bridges Press, New York

McGrath, J. F., 2001, *John's Apologetic Christology: Legitimation and Development in Johannine Christology*, Cambridge University Press, Cambridge

McGrath & Newell, P. & C., 2004, 'The Human Connection: A Case Study of Spirituality and Disability', *Newell & Calder, op cit*

Milbank, J., 1999, 'The Ethics of Self-Sacrifice ', *First Things*, 91, March

Monteith, W. G., 2005, *Deconstructing Miracles*, Covenanter Press, Glasgow

Newell & Calder, C. & A., 2004, *Voices in Disability and Spirituality from the Land Down Under*, Haworth Pastoral Press, Binghamton, NY

Newlands, G. M., 2003, *Christ and Human Rights: The Transformative Engagement*, Ashgate Publishing, Burlington, VT

Njoroge, N., 1997, 'Woman, Why Are You Weeping?, *The Ecumenical Review*, Vol 49, No 4

Norenzayan, et al, A., 2008, 'The Origin and Evolution of Religious Prosociality', *Science*, Vol 322, No 58

Nussbaum, M. C., 2006, *Frontiers of Justice*, Belknap Press, Cambridge, Mass.

Ochs, R., 1969, *The Death in Every Now*, Sheed and Ward, New York

Pilch, J. J., 1995, *The Cultural World of Jesus*, Liturgical Press, Collegeville, Min.

Rawls, J., 1971, *Theory of Justice*, Harvard University Press, Cambridge, Mass.

Reinders, H. S., 2008, *Receiving the Gift of Friendship*, Wm B Eerdmans, Grand Rapids

Reynolds, T. E., 2008, *Vulnerable Communion: A Theology of Disability and Hospitality*, Brazos Press, Grand Rapids

Sandman, L., 2005, *Good Death: On the Value of Death and Dying*, Open University Press, London

Saunders, F. S., 2003, 'T S Eliot Wept Here, While Thomas Mann Wrote a Novel about a Man with a Hacking Cough. A Good Place to Die?', *New Statesman*, 132, 4635, April 28

Schlessinger, L., 1989, *The Ten Commandments: the significance of God's laws in everyday life*, Cliff Street Books, New York

Shapin & Martyn, S. & C., 2000, 'How to live forever: lessons of history', *British Medical Journal*, 321

Singer, P., 2002, *Unsanctifying Human Life*, Blackwell, Oxford

Somerville, M. A., 2002, *Death Talk: The Case Against Euthanasia and Physician-Assisted Suicide*, McGill-Queen's University Press, Montreal

Swinton, J., 2001, *Resurrecting the Person*, Abington Press, Nashville

Thomas, D., 1976, *Selected Works*, Book Club Associates, London

Vanier, J., 1998, *The scandal of service: Jesus washes our feet*, Novalis, Toronto

Voragine, J., 1260/1993, *The golden legend: readings on the saints; translated by William Granger Ryan*, Princeton University Press, Princeton, NJ

Walls, J. L., 2002, *Heaven: The Logic of Eternal Joy*, Oxford University Press, New York

Walter, T., 1994, *The Revival of Death*, Routledge, New York

BIBLIOGRAPHY

Webster, J., 2000, *The Cambridge Companion to Karl Barth*, Cambridge University Press, Cambridge

Westbrook *et al*, R., 2003, *A History of Ancient Near Eastern Law. Volume: 2*, Brill, Leiden

Yong, A., 2007, *Theology and Down Syndrome: reimagining disability in late modernity*, Baylor University Press, Waco, Tex.

Young, J., 2003, *The Death of God and the Meaning of Life*, Routledge, London

Lightning Source UK Ltd.
Milton Keynes UK
27 November 2010

163526UK00002B/1/P